Family
TIES

RESTORING UNITY IN THE
AFRICAN AMERICAN FAMILY

COLLEEN BIRCHETT, PH.D.

UMI (Urban Ministries, Inc.)
Chicago, Illinois

Publisher
UMI (Urban Ministries, Inc.)
P.O. Box 436987
Chicago, IL 60643-6987
1-800-860-8642
www.urbanministries.com

First Edition
First Printing

Unless otherwise noted, Scriptures are taken from the *HOLY BIBLE, NEW INTERNATIONAL VERSION* ® . Copyright © 1973, 1978, 1984 by International Bible Society. Used by permission of Zondervan Publishing House. All rights reserved.

Library of Congress Cataloging-in-Publication Data

    Family ties—restoring unity in the African American family / Colleen Birchett.
    Includes bibliographical references.
    ISBN 01-932715-69-X
    ISBN 978-1-932715-69-9
    1. Family and relationships. 2. Christian living. 3. African American families—religious life.
    I. Title.

Library of Congress Control Number: 2006902649

Printed in the United States of America.

TABLE OF CONTENTS

ACKNOWLEDGMENTS

I must take the time to thank several people, without whom this book would not have come into being. I am very grateful for the critique, guidance, and inspiration of Dr. Hal Taussig, professor of New Testament at Union Theological Seminary. In the midst of teaching classes and pastoring an African American church, he took the time to read the entire manuscript and make very helpful suggestions. He also encouraged and affirmed me concerning the overall worth of the project. I also want to thank Frances Harris, Superintendent of Church School at Trinity United Church of Christ in Chicago for "brainstorming sessions" we conducted between Chicago and New York—sessions that surfaced some of the content for various chapters and introductory stories.

I thank professors at Union Theological Seminary who gave me extensions so that I could complete the book during the last weeks of December 2005. These wonderful people are: Professors Esther Hamori, Karen Jones, Janet Walton, Troy Messenger, Barbara Lundblad, and Dean Euan Cameron, who gave final approval for the extension requests.

Of course, ultimately, without my family's support, I would not be the person that I am, nor would I have the spiritual insights that shaped the book. First and foremost, I want to thank my parents, Esther Birchett and Wilbur Birchett. I want to thank, in particular, my sister, Jalna Birchett-Hayes, and my brothers Wilbur, Michael, David, Anthony, Patrick, Ishan Dan, and Derrick. I would like to express appreciation to my brother-in-law Clarence Hayes, and to each of my brothers' wives: Clarisene, Diane, Diana, Andrea, and Jodie. In addition, I thank my aunts, Barbara and Renelda, and also Steen, Juanita, Maggie, Rosalee, Barbara, and Jerry. I want to thank my uncles, Harold, Kent, and Andrew, along with all of my nieces, nephews, and cousins. Of course, I also want to express appreciation for all of the family members, on both sides of my family, who have gone to be with the Lord.

I wish to thank C. Jeffrey Wright, J.D., president and CEO of UMI and Dr. Melvin E. Banks Sr., founder and chairman of UMI, for the invitation to write the book. I also thank them for publishing the eight other Bible studies that I compiled. I also wish to thank Dr. Cheryl Clemetson, Director of Editorial, and Kathryn Hall, Managing Editor, for their patience and assistance throughout the development of the book.

I wish to thank Dr. Jeremiah A. Wright, my pastor at Trinity United Church of Christ in Chicago, for his constant inspiration and encouragement, along with my Trinity family, in particular the Hurston-Hughes Writers who have been a constant source of inspiration to me. I wish to thank Dr. James Forbes of Riverside Church in New York, who is my dynamic and poetic pastor away from home, while I am completing studies at Union Theological Seminary in New York. Finally, I wish to thank Patricia Ashby, whose professional skills helped me to begin locating my personal voice for ministry.

PREFACE

The achievement of this set of Bible studies is difficult to put into proper perspective. To my mind, it stands in the top five Bible study guides for laypersons ever published. Moreover, this work—in my sincerest hopes—can become a model for the way Bible study material for laypersons should be written and published for the foreseeable future.

There are four major reasons for these superlatives for this work:

1. The ways in which the stories of real families and individuals in our time are woven into the fabric of the Bible stories is an extraordinary model for how the Bible needs to function in our lives. Bible stories were written so that our lives may be woven into them, and that our identities may be formed through this interweaving of stories. Here the Bible story begets our telling of who we are, and then our telling of our stories in relationship to the Bible story begets a new understanding of who we are. The looping of story into story lets us be held in the weave of sacred writ. It goes beyond the intuition of devotional literature and presents whole stories laced together into an even greater whole.

2. The way in which each chapter's "Closer Look" at both our contemporary stories and the biblical stories deepen the interwoven unity demonstrates the virtue of real Bible study. Here new and important information about both our own lives and biblical times help us see how the two are related. This deepening process of Bible study manifests itself here in stunning contrast to the staid recounting of what the reader already knows. This material resonates with solid, interesting, and new information. It invites those studying the Bible to want to learn more about both the Bible and themselves.

3. The bringing to light the many dimensions of African American life in each chapter breaks important new ground in the recognition of the ways African American truth invites encounters with the Bible. The erasure of African American lives from Bible study material in United States culture has lessened a major lens through which we can see biblical truth. This book begins remedy with winsome writing and penetrating research.

4. Perhaps most of all, this set of studies shows us why Bible study is best done when in explicit dialogue with a specific cultural reality of our day. It reveals how the specificity of real-life settings of our day do justice to the biblical portrait of a God that cares about history. Far more engaging and revealing than the generalizations of commentaries, this book claims an incarnational form, in which the revelation of God takes flesh in our lives.

Colleen Birchett has given us a major tool for understanding ourselves, the Bible, and the importance of African American faith. We are deeply in her debt.

Hal Taussig
Visiting Professor of New Testament
Union Theological Seminary

INTRODUCTION

It was my Uncle Jacky's funeral. I sat near the aisle in the fifth row, with my eyes panning across the room. Aunts, uncles, cousins, brothers, nieces, nephews, my sister, and our friends were all there. Collectively, it was both loss and renewal that we had come to this place to share. As I sat listening to my brother Elder David Birchett share the stories of our childhood as they related to my uncle, I seemed to have an appreciation for these stories that was greater than ever before.

These were the stories of how we, as an extended family, got over. These were the stories that had united us under God. As one relative after another got up and shared their stories, it suddenly impressed me that Someone much greater than any of us had tied these stories together. Upon close examination, this was one overall saga of one extended family's struggle to survive, and its struggle was based on a core set of Christian values that had, at some point of the family's history, been learned from the Bible itself.

There was the story of how my grandmother, in a wheelchair, had raised 12 children. There was the story of how my mother had raised nine children, along with caring for an ailing husband. There were the stories of my brothers and uncles who had gone away and come back from war, and there were the stories of how, when our father was too sick to care for us, our uncles, such as Uncle Jacky, had helped my mother and my grandmother. There were the stories of our aunts and uncles taking us to church, and how we stayed at church all day.

Then, after the funeral, and after the return from the cemetery, as usual, we all promised one another that we would organize that great family reunion that was way overdue. We promised to try to see each other more often, and we exchanged telephone numbers with those whose telephone numbers we had lost.

However, in reality, no one could deny that this family itself had actually become fragmented over time. As I rode back home on the plane to New

York, I kept telling myself that something needs to be done. There must be some way to reunite this family, even over the miles. There must be untapped resources for achieving this. In fact, my mind even wandered to the possibility of a family corporation, where our collective resources could be stored and tapped when necessary. I thought of the family genealogy that isolated family members had been compiling, but, as yet, had not shared. Where were all those family pictures? Who really had them, or were they lost?

Of course, eventually my mind traveled to the families of the Bible. I thought of the families of which Norman Gottwald calls, the "Tribes of Yahweh"—the Israelites living within the context of one empire after another, yet developing a family system that helped them to pool their resources, and to whom God revealed timeless principles and values for resisting the divisive influences of the empires that surrounded them. I thought of their covenant with God, and God's covenant with African Americans. I thought of the central role of the temple in Israel, and the central role of the African American church in the struggle of African Americans. Were these not resources that our family could use in twenty-first century America?

When I got back to New York, I began preparations to write this book, with the question of: What were the values that helped Israel's families to survive, unite, repair, and reunite, in the wide variety of circumstances in which they found themselves in both the Old and New Testaments?

The resulting book, *Family Ties: Restoring Unity in the African American Family*, contains vignettes from a collection of Bible families, paired with vignettes from African American family life. **While the vignettes are not stories from my personal family life, each chapter illustrates timeless values that have proven to renew and reunite nuclear and extended families everywhere.**

The book provides the opportunity to study and reflect upon these stories and to apply the principles gleaned to reuniting and reinvigorating families. Each chapter is devoted to a different principle. Each chapter begins with a vignette/case study from African American family life paired with a similar story from the Bible. Each chapter presents background information on the historical context of the Bible family and guidance in drawing insights for modern applications.

The overriding theme throughout is the role that Jesus, the Son of God, the great Unifier, Savior, Redeemer, and Lord, has been and is the primary resource for creating and reuniting Christian families. The book emphasizes the miracle of rebirth, and how that rebirth and resurrection become recurring themes throughout personal and collective time. The book also reiterates the futility of trying to achieve unity and/or strength in the nuclear or in the extended family without this spiritual basis.

The following is an adaptation from a sermon preached by my pastor, Dr. Jeremiah A. Wright Jr., entitled, "What's Wrong with My Family?" The message is an excellent introduction to the subject of this book, which addresses the natural and spiritual issues surrounding the need to restore unity in the African American family structure. As you read, allow God to minister healing to you as you seek answers regarding the needs of your family, your church, and your community.

"What's Wrong with My Family?"
By Dr. Jeremiah A. Wright Jr.

"May God arise, may his enemies be scattered; may his foes flee before him. But may the righteous be glad and rejoice before God; may they be happy and joyful. Sing to God, sing praise to his name, extol him who rides on the clouds—his name is the LORD—and rejoice before him. A father to the fatherless, a defender of widows, is God in his holy dwelling. God sets the lonely in families…" (Psalm 68:1, 3–6, NIV).

Psalm 68 begins by celebrating and singing praises to God for [some good] reasons. The songwriter then says that God is to be praised because of His name—in other words for His name's sake. God is to be praised because His name is the Lord. Here the songwriter uses the same word as in Exodus 6:2–3, where God says to Moses, "I am the LORD. I appeared to Abraham, to Isaac and to Jacob as God Almighty, but by my name the LORD I did not make myself known to them." In other words, God is to be praised because His name is "I Am that I Am." I will be what I will be.

Jesus put it this way: "Before Abraham was born, I am. To those who are hungry, I am. I am the Bread of Life. To those who are thirsty, I am. I am the Living Water. To those who are lost in darkness, I am the Light of the World. I am the Way, the Truth and the Life. To those who have lost loved ones, and who are wrestling with grief, and who feel dead on the inside, I am the resurrection and the life." God is to be praised because His name is I am. God is to be praised for His name's sake.

When was the last time you praised God just because of His name? Lord, God Almighty, Lord of Abraham and Sarah, Lord of Isaac and Rebecca, Lord of Jacob and Rachel, Lord of Henry Turner and Harriet Tubman, Lord of Martin and Coretta, Lord in a lion's den and a fiery furnace, Lord who's a wheel in the middle of a wheel, and fire shut up in your bones. Lord, Matthew's burden bearer, Luke's heavy load sharer, John's heart fixer, and Mark's mind regulator. Lord, Joshua's battle ax, Moses' burning bush, Abraham's ram. In the thick, it's Mary's sweet little Jesus boy.

Then the writer picks up a theme from way back in Genesis 2 and says we ought to praise God because He is a God of community, a God of covenant, and a God who cares. He does not allow those who are alone to be lonely. He looks out for widows, orphans, and those with no place to call home. God cares for those who have been deserted, those who have been devastated by death and those who have been left desolate. He's a mother to the motherless; He is a father to the fatherless. I know some Black children who need to hear and learn this Psalm. He is a defender of the widows, and the lonely He sets in families. It is not God's intention or desire for us to pass from the cradle to the grave in isolation. We are created to be in relationship with others of God's creatures. God's design is for us to be a part of a family. I need a family, no matter what that configuration of family might be.

I need Mama and my auntie, and Big Mama, and Ma'Dear. I need a mother figure, even if it's not my natural mother. I need Daddy and Grandpa, men in my life, even if it's not my natural daddy. I need to be in community and in covenant in order to learn about caring. It is God's design for me to be a part of a family. God decided that it was not good for man [or for woman] to be alone. So He made them a family to be in relationship with.

Genesis 2:18–24 conceptualizes how God intended for this thing to be. It's really an expansion of Genesis 1:26–28, which says that God was already in community, living as one in the Trinity: God the Father, God the Son, and God the Holy Spirit. God said, "Let us make man in our image, in our likeness, and let them rule over the fish of the sea and the birds of the air, [and the animals]....So God created man in his own image." We were created in community, formed for fellowship, and brought into being as already a part of a family—that was God's design.

When a newborn baby is born, that baby's personality is yet to be complete. Creation does not crown the child until the name is given.

Initially, this takes place unofficially or sociologically in the hospital. It takes place officially and theologically in the church where the baby is given its Christian name. That's why the preacher says to call the child's name. It's when that name is pronounced in the context of a Christian community that that baby becomes a real person. When you give something or someone its name, you participate in the act of creation.

Seven hundred years before Jesus' birth, a holy word from heaven was given to the prophet Isaiah. His name shall be Wonderful Counselor, the Mighty God, the Everlasting Father, the Prince of Peace, Emmanuel, or God with us. Then a holy messenger was sent by his daddy's house to tell him to call his name Jesus, because he shall save His people from their sin. Jesus is not named in the human community until Joseph pronounces that name in the temple. John the Baptist is not named in the human community until Zachariah pronounces his name in the temple. Samuel is not named in the human community until Elkanah pronounces his name in the temple. When you can pronounce a person's name, it symbolizes the power that you have over that person as a co-creator, or one who participates in their creation.

It takes another person for us to be in fellowship and in relationship. Family is where we learn how to love. Family is where we learn how to share. Family is where we learn how to forgive. Family is where we learn what it means to be accepted, not because of what we do, but because of who we are. Family is God's design for human community, whether it's a single-parent family or an extended family. That is God's design for our good will.

In order for a house to be a home, love has got to be there—love that is bigger than the mistakes we make; love that outlives the differences and the disagreements; and love that forms us, reforms us, and transforms us. Love is God's anecdote for loneliness; family is God's design for human community. Family is where I find out who I am. I get my primary definition of self from the family.

Family is where I first find out who God is. I get my primary understanding of my Heavenly Father from my family. If God is important, I learn that from my family long before I get to the church. If God is not important, I also learn that from my family long before I get to the church. If nobody prays at home, if nobody reads Scripture at home, if nobody talks about how good God has been at home, and if nobody sings about His mercy and His grace at home, then I know it's not important. That is the primary understanding I will have long before I get to school or to church.

Family is where I find out who I am and family is where I find out who God is. Then family is where I find out what love is—love that accepts me for what I am and love that holds on to me while I am becoming what God meant for me to be. It's a love that wipes away the bruises inflicted by a racist society and bruises inflicted by a self-hatred syndrome that continues to see itself through the eyes of others. It's a love that clears that up, that picks me up when I've been knocked down, and holds me up when I've been put down.

A young man once asked me, "If all of this is true, then what's wrong with my family? Why is my family so messed up? Why is my family so far away from God's design for the human community?" As he asked the question, "What's wrong with my family?" it was an eerie feeling because I have heard so many people asking that same question and I've heard myself asking the same question: "what's wrong with my family?"

Someone told me that they have members of their family using dope, while another says they've got members of their family selling dope. What's wrong with my family? One person has a brother they don't speak to all year long and another has a sister they can't stand. One family has a mental patient keeping everybody confused, and another family has a liar that no one can trust. One family has a "stuff stirrer upper" who isn't happy unless they're stirring something up. One family has a child who refuses to go to school; another family has a husband who refuses to go to work. One family has a 40-year-old still sleeping at home and another family has a 14-year-old sleeping everywhere but at home. One family has a father who acts like a fool; another family's got a mama who is a complete fool.

Now I don't care how powerful and perfect you think your family is; somewhere in that family tree there's somebody that nobody likes to talk about that much. One little second grader said to me, "Reverend Wright, why can't my mommy and my daddy live in the same house and sleep in the same bed? Why does my family have to be in two places like that?"

All of our families have problems and all of the biblical families had problems. In pre-history Adam and Eve had one son who killed the other son. Then Noah, for all his faithfulness, had a drinking problem. He became intoxicated, pulled off all his clothes, and passed out. What's wrong with my family? Starting in Genesis 12 and running all the way to the New Testament, every family you run across had a problem. Do you want to be part of Abraham's family? Abraham did not protect his own wife. He caused

Hagar to be a single parent trying to raise Abraham's son all by herself, without child support. What's wrong with my family?

Do you want to be a part of Isaac's family? Isaac's son, Esau, had two wives who made life miserable for their mother-in-law. Do you want to be a part of Jacob's family? Jacob lied to his daddy, tricked his brother, had babies by four women, and was in a conspiracy with his mother. Joseph was doted on by his father and hated by his brothers. Moses was a murderer. He was a fugitive from justice, with a brother and a sister who couldn't stand his Black wife. Do you want to be a part of Samuel's family? Samuel had a daddy who had a second family living in the same house with his mother. And then his own sons brought him nothing but misery. Do you want to be a part of Saul's family? Saul was schizophrenic and manic depressive. One day he loved David, and the next day he was throwing a spear at him. Saul's daughter was married to David and his son was his best friend, and Saul hated David's guts. Do you want to be a part of David's family? David had one son who hated another son because that son raped David's daughter. David had one wife that he was going with before she got a divorce and got her pregnant while her husband was still alive. He had one of his children kill another one of his children. Then his own son tried to rip him off while his other sons fought over his estate before his body got cold. Do you want to be a part of that family? Solomon had so many outside women that he lost count. His sons fell out before he was cold and split the kingdom in two. Hosea was married to a whore.

Jesus had a family that thought he had lost His mind. His best friend Lazarus had two sisters who fought like cats and dogs. Where do you find this ideal family that everybody keeps talking about? To be a human means you've got problems. Nothing is perfect—no relationship, no church, and no family. What's wrong with your family? Nothing. It's normal, that's all. It's natural, that's all—and it needs God, that's all, because no one is perfect, except God.

Our families need God. We need God. God is the only constant in a swirling sea of inconsistencies. God is the joy and the strength of life. God is the one who moves misery and strife. God is the one who promises to keep you and never leave you. God is the one who never, ever comes short of His Word. God is the one who can stand in the midst of our families and make a way out of no way. He can turn tears into laughter, turn sadness into joy, bring community out of chaos, and take a crooked stick and hit a straight lick. God is our all in all.

If you, or someone that you know, are outside of the family of God, know that the Lord Jesus Christ has extended an invitation: "Come unto me, all ye that labor and are heavy laden." Thank You, God, for putting us in families. Thank you, God, for making us a part of Your great family. You are the one constant factor in our lives, when our families are celebrating, gathering around a grave tomb, or sitting at a dinner table. Know that God is always present.

© Sermon copyrighted by Rev. Dr. Jeremiah A. Wright Jr.

STARTING OVER VS. REMAINING THE SAME

Nicodemus: John 3:1–16; 7:37–52; 19:37–42

It was Thursday. The family reunion would begin on Friday night, so Ann had been working all day to get everything ready.

In a way, she thought, she was looking forward to the reunion, but in another way, she was a little nervous. Things had really changed in her life, but she didn't know whether her family was ready for it. She didn't know whether they would believe her, or understand.

As she sat there braiding her youngest daughter's hair, her mind went back to the day that when it seems the problems that had become part of her testimony all began. She had just turned 12 years old—about the age her oldest daughter was now. Her body had begun to change, and her mother had told her that she was now a young woman. She recalled, even then, that her attention had already turned to boys. She had become very curious about sex. By the time that she turned 15, she had become pregnant. She would never forget the way that her mother had found out about it. The boy that she had been sleeping with had been bragging about her in the boys' locker room at school, and her older brother, Carl, heard it and had gotten into a fight.

Angry, Carl had confronted Ann on their way home from school. He told her how embarrassed he was, because he was a Christian and he didn't want people knowing that he had a little sister who was already pregnant. When they had gotten home, he went straight into the kitchen and told their mother. The news soon began to spread all over the family. That was just the beginning of the gossip. It seemed that the "grapevine" had always carried news of what was going on with Ann. Her extended family knew about her breakup with her child's father, her second child born out of wedlock, how she finally left her home because she couldn't get along with her brother Carl, and even that she had signed up for welfare assistance.

And yes, the family found out about how she had married an older man, thinking that he would support her and her children, only to be continually beaten up by him. She remembered how her mother had come to rescue her and the children from the shelter where she had fled. However, it had not been long before Ann had moved across town, in an effort to keep her business to herself. She was surprised to have received a call from Angela, inviting her to the family reunion. She really had to ask herself whether she wanted to start over with her family, or leave things as they were.

This wasn't the first time that she'd had to make such a decision.

She recalled when she finally decided to accept Christ as her personal Savior. It was around the time that she had found a part-time job at the local grocery store. The money from the job added to what she was getting from the welfare department. Ann had been proud of herself, because it was very difficult to get a job if a person hadn't finished high school. When she learned that she got the job, she surprised herself by saying, "Praise the Lord!"—a phrase she hadn't heard since it came out of her Aunt Emma's mouth when she was a little girl.

At the store, she had become friends with her coworker Charlene. Charlene took her children to church, and was always thanking God for something or the other. She had always tried to find the positive side when unfortunate things happened to her or to her children.

Charlene had been inviting Ann to join her church. *I wish she would quit bothering me about that*, Ann had thought. But one day Charlene asked Ann to come to her church to see her children participate in a Church School program. Charlene's children were friends with her children, but churches turned her off. She had been staying away from them on purpose. They reminded her too much of her family. She recalled, with anger, how all her family seemed to do was talk about her. She never recalled anyone inviting her to church. *They don't want me around their church friends because I am a so-called "unwed mother,"* she thought. *They're nothing but a bunch of hypocrites.*

And then again, she didn't want to join some church that would interfere with her new relationship with a man she had met at the store. This had the potential to be a good thing for her. On the other hand, she really wanted to see Charlene's children in the play. So she went. She and her children enjoyed the program so much that they had decided to stay for church, if for no other reason than to get a ride home with Charlene.

She would never forget the sermon that was delivered that Sunday morning. It was about the woman that Jesus met at the well in the fourth chapter of the gospel of John. The pastor had talked about the pain that the woman must have felt, looking for love in all the wrong places. He talked about how Jesus had seen beyond all the mistakes that this woman had made, to meet this woman's need—the need to be loved. He talked about how God was creating a new family that included people just like this woman at the well.

God knew everything that had happened to her and loved her just the same. The pastor spoke about how everyone in the town must have been talking about this woman. Nobody would be found talking in public with a woman like her. But Jesus was not ashamed of her. Jesus would talk to her when nobody else would. In fact, God had something for this woman to do. The woman had to decide whether she wanted to change and start all over again, or whether she wanted to remain the same. The pastor told how once the woman had a little talk with Jesus, she decided to change, and she did what God had called her to do with great enthusiasm!

At the end of the sermon, the pastor had held out his hand and had asked anyone who wanted to walk forward, give the pastor his or her hand, and give Jesus his or her heart. Ann asked herself, *Do I want to start over, just like this woman at the well, or do I want things to remain the same?* On the spur of the moment, Ann's feet seemed to have a life of their own. Before she knew it, she was standing before the altar, giving Jesus her heart.

Since that day, she and her children had become a part of this church family. She had learned so much about the Bible and about her African heritage. Her children sang in the children's choir and she sang in the adult choir. She had also become a clerk in the Church School, and she had enrolled in the G.E.D. classes that the local high school held at the church.

Today, she sat a new person, braiding her daughters' hair, and considering whether to face her family again. On the television Gospel show, Yolanda Adams was singing, "A Wonderful Change Has Come Over Me!" Once again, she had a decision to make. Did she really want to start over with her family, or would she rather leave things as they were? She decided to start over. And *even if their attitudes remain the same,* she thought, *the important thing is that I am different. Now I am the person that God made me to be. That will not change.*

A CLOSER LOOK

Ann, in the introductory story, underwent a process of change that is certainly not foreign to the African American community. It is the type of situation that has been repeated in many places, in many times, and with many people. Difficult situations can have a life of their own. In and of themselves, they can "take the driver's seat," and cause a sense of powerlessness. Such situations contain negative messages that can be internalized by the persons affected. Moreover, wrong decisions can exacerbate matters, bring unfair judgments and rejection from others, and possibly trigger a downward spiral. Unfortunately, in these circumstances, such an individual can ignore the voice of God calling the person to reach out to God. For it is God who helps us to see ourselves in a different way—as made in the image of God. This change does happen when a person accepts Jesus Christ as his or her personal Savior, and decides to start all over again. Ann's and Nicodemus's stories are parallel in this respect.

Like so many other situations within the African American community, one has to look closer at Ann's situation in order to identify the aspects of it that may certainly have been imposed from outside. For example, for a number of years now, researchers have been trying to answer the question of why so many African American girls are entering puberty at increasingly earlier ages. There are theories about the food that is sold in urban areas possibly containing lower-quality ingredients. There are theories that the changes in development may be related to the fact that a significant percentage of African Americans live near toxic dump waste sites (Pinn 2002, 83). Moreover, for some girls, other factors have to be accounted for, such as sexual abuse. Whatever the case, what may have been an external factor, related to the maturity of a young girls' body, may also have been aggravated by her wrong choices. The problems that resulted created yet another challenge—the need to redefine oneself as a child of God.

Theologian Dr. Dwight Hopkins, of the University of Chicago, in his book, *Down, Up, and Over: Slave Religion and Black Theology*, describes a very similar process taking place among Africans who had been stolen from Africa and sold as slaves in the Western hemisphere. External circumstances would have told them that they were not human at all. Slavery was a circumstance that was designed to overwhelm, and produce powerlessness and docility. It was not designed to foster a sense, in the slaves, that they were made in the image of God (Hopkins 1999, 25–26). What could such a person have thought of him or herself if that individual had internalized the negativity that was being thrust upon him or her by the slave system? As individuals, they had been gathered into groups and taken from Africa, chained to the floors of slave ships. They had been brought across the Atlantic Ocean and then sold, mostly naked, on auction blocks. They had been forced to give free labor to White people for the remainder of most of their lives (Dunaway 2003, 18).

However, even in the midst of this, there was the voice of God. On the plantations to which they were eventually sold, these same slaves "held church" in the middle of the night, outside of the views of the slave masters. In the "hush harbors" of the "invisible institutions" (the Black church), these Africans rejected the negative messages that had come to them by way of the plantation system and the people who ran it. They rejected the messages that they were not valuable persons. Instead, they "had a little talk with Jesus" in the middle of the night and Jesus made it all right for them. They came away with a new image of themselves, and indeed with this new image, many even gained the courage to run away, conduct slave revolts, raise the money to purchase freedom for themselves and for their family members, fight for their freedom in the courts, and return South over and over to liberate others and/or to just resist their plight by keeping an image of themselves within themselves that said that they were not really slaves, but people of God, held in bondage (Dunaway 2003, 51).

This ability to draw strength from having a relationship with Jesus where by our ancestors saw themselves as God saw them also became a part of the culture of the early African American church, a feature that has been passed on to us, and that was extended to Ann in the introductory story. As she sat at the back of the church that Sunday morning, Ann responded to the story of how the biblical woman at the well had drawn strength from her encounter with Jesus, received a new image of herself, and had subsequently become an ambassador for Christ. It is a parallel process that caused Ann to have a little talk with Jesus, who helped her reimage herself from a seemingly hopeless victim of bad relationships and abuse to an African Queen working on behalf of God's kingdom.

Hopkins explains that the slaves had used the methods of the Black self that were available to them in God to "redraw the boundaries between externally imposed definitions and internally initiated lifestyles grounded in fundamental faith claims" (Hopkins 1999, 108). He says: "To know oneself and to take care of oneself was to release the enthusiasm in determining how one wanted to be in the world along with a God who liberates one from an old self and frees one to a new self" (115).

The process that Hopkins describes is not frozen in time. In churches and in personal relationships throughout the country, God's voice speaks, extending this invitation to take care of oneself, by establishing a "holy hookup" with God. That is where it begins. The energy of the Holy Spirit then releases enthusiasm within the person. In boldness the person can decide, with God's help, who he or she wants to be "in the face" of all who send out contrary messages. In bold defiance, people like Ann, Charlene, our ancestors, and Nicodemus are all able to take off the old self and enter the new—in broad daylight!

However, as can be seen in Ann's story, the process does not begin and end with the individual. Hopkins explains how the individual salvation event occurs in community and impacts the community: "Moreover, this freeing spiritual presence works with us in the co-constitution of the new African American self; that is to say, in the ongoing creation narrative of divine-poor co-laboring for a new common wealth on earth" (Hopkins 1999, 194).

Once Ann recognized who she really was, immediately she was drawn into the church family/community where she discovered how her gifts can help others and build up the general community, creating sacred space for others to make the same journey to God-awareness and self-awareness that she had made. There is no promise that all troubles will disappear, or that there will not be cause to mourn. However, as Hopkins puts it, "Joy, with the poor in their mournful state, comes from Jesus" (Hopkins 1999, 195). As Ann and her children take up their places in the community of faith, God's kingdom on Earth, this "entails the giving of power from Jesus to those who accept the call and the power to servant hood for the least in society" (196).

"Faith lets the poor know that trouble does not last always. And despite all appearances of persistent excruciating pain internally and formidable oppressive systems externally, the least in society know how Jesus is with them through the resurrection's victory over the death of poverty and pain" (Hopkins 1999, 201).

Coming to God for salvation and refreshment is promoted in the Bible, and in Christian churches everywhere. This process is certainly one of the resources promoted in the African American church. Anthony Pinn, in *The Black Church in the Post-Civil Rights Era* references Barna research that reports: Of the African Americans surveyed (34 million), 94% said they prayed to God within that past week. Forty-nine percent (27 million) said that they considered themselves "spiritual" and 61% (roughly 20 million) considered themselves "committed and born-again Christians" (Pinn 2002, xii, http://www/barna.org). Why? They say it is because what happens during the worship service affects both their behavior and outlook during the following week. Considering other reports of negative environmental factors in the lives of African Americans, it is likely that salvation and refinement are ongoing events that are occurring within the church/family communities.

A CLOSER LOOK AT NICODEMUS
John 3:1–16; 7:37–52; 19:37–42

John 3:1 Now there was a man of the Pharisees named Nicodemus, a member of the Jewish ruling council. **2** He came to Jesus at night and said, "Rabbi, we know you are a teacher who has come from God. For no one could perform the miraculous signs you are doing if God were not with him." **3** In reply Jesus declared, "I tell you the truth, no one can see the kingdom of God unless he is born again." **4** "How can a man be born when he is old?" Nicodemus asked. "Surely he cannot enter a second time into his mother's womb to be born!" **5** Jesus answered, "I tell you the truth, no one can enter the kingdom of God unless he is born or water and the Spirit. **6** Flesh gives birth to flesh, but the Spirit gives birth to spirit. **7** You should not be surprised at my saying, 'You must be born again.' **8** The wind blows wherever it pleases. You hear its sound, but you cannot tell where it comes from or where it is going. So it is with everyone born of the Spirit." (See also John 3:9–16; 7:37–52; 19:37–42.)

There are many parallels between Ann's story (in the introductory story) and that of Nicodemus in the third chapter of John. While one can only speculate, from all indications, Nicodemus, too, seems to have been born into an environment with factors that could possibly have resulted in his having an image of himself that was different from the one that God wanted for him. The image of an aristocrat in those days was one who was corrupt, violent, and abusive of the poor (Horsley 2003, 20). The image of a member of the Sanhedrin was that of an aristocrat who bent the Mosaic Laws in order to satisfy the Roman government on the one hand, and to become rich on the other (35). Within that environment, it is possible that Nicodemus, too, could have made poor choices. Whatever the case, eventually he, in a manner similar to Ann's experience, heard the voice of God, speaking through God's Son, Jesus Christ. Moreover, Scripture carries more than a hint that Nicodemus also changed, after he had a little talk with Jesus. In Nicodemus' situation, the change became evident as he went from sneaking around and questioning Jesus in the dark to associating himself with Jesus in broad daylight (see John 19:39)!

Scholars such as Richard Horsley, in *Jesus and Empire*, assert that, at the time of Christ, sustaining one's wealth at a given level meant that a person would have needed to engage in some degree of defrauding the poor (Horsley 2003, 123). Even Jesus had said that it would be easier for a camel to pass through the eye of a needle than for a rich person to get into heaven (see Matthew 19:24). Within the structure of the Roman economy, it was common practice for aristocrats to maintain their wealth by either exploiting the vulnerable in some way, or by being a beneficiary of a family system that had gained its wealth by defrauding the poor. Moreover, during the time prior to this biblical account, there had already been centuries of corruption, violence, wars, and class conflict involving administrators within the temple at Jerusalem . The leftovers of these conflicts had resulted in three major aspects of Judaism: the Pharisees, Essenes, and Sadducees. These factors coexisted with various messianic, zealot, and Jewish terrorists groups (Koester 1987, 94). More than likely, Nicodemus would have been situated in the midst of all this.

The poor and vulnerable were peasants, who constituted the majority of the population in Galilee—the region where Jesus grew up and ministered. Such people were either in constant danger of losing their land and/or were in a type of sharecropping arrangement where they existed for the purpose of growing cash crops to pay their taxes and to survive. The Roman and Jewish aristocrats could have easily taken advantage of such people by charging the vulnerable higher interest, foreclosing on their lands, and selling their property (Horsley 2003, 123). Some aristocrats even gained land by marrying and divorcing wives—collecting dowries and then either killing their wives or divorcing them, plunging the women into poverty (Satlow 1993, 133).

In fact, the vulnerable were required to pay multi-tiers of taxes—to the Roman government, to the temple in Jerusalem, and to King Herod. Moreover, they were also likely to become victims of the publicans or the temple personnel, the professional tax collectors who were hired out by Rome, Herod, and/or the aristocrats. Such collectors were unpopular because they inflated the amount owed in order to earn maximum personal profits at the expense of the poor. Moreover, the amount of taxes owed did not vary based on rises and falls in crop yields due to natural disasters and famines.

In terms of environment, from all indications, the context in which Nicodemus surfaces on the pages of Scripture is one of wealth and corruption. No doubt Nicodemus was born into a generation that was, by then, an intimate part of this abusive, oppressive, and violent system. To maintain his status, he possibly would have benefited from and/or participated in this system in some manner. For example, Nicodemus himself was a wealthy Pharisee. He was not just any Pharisee, but a leader of the Jews. He was part of the ruling class.

However, as he observed rampant corruption in the society in which he existed and the problems of the vulnerable throughout Palestine, Nicodemus may have been seeking answers. Conceivably, Jesus was one of the people whom he studied from a distance. Was he a quiet listener in some of the groups of Pharisees who are found in Scripture posing various questions to Jesus? If Nicodemus was a member of the Jerusalem Sanhedrin and/or a member of a lesser Sanhedrin in Galilee, and/or frequented one of the synagogues in the region where Jesus had appeared, he might have been a little more than fascinated by what Jesus was saying. Given the accuracy of these assumptions, through Jesus' words, Nicodemus would have recognized a different voice, an alternative message that spoke about an image of the person that he would like to be.

If he questioned his existence at all, as a Pharisee and as a member of the Sanhedrin, he would also have realized that he was "caught in the middle"—in that, he had to "go along to get along" on some level. But, as a Pharisee, with the reputation of being well aware of the social justice aspects of the Law in particular (such as the Year of Jubilee), Nicodemus might have been able to see conflicts between the practices and decisions of his colleagues on the Sanhedrin (Sadduccees as well as Pharisees) and the social justice aspects of the Mosaic Law (see Leviticus 25).

Richard Horsley and John Dominic Crossan both indicate how the temple interpreters of the law often bent the law in order to accommodate economic and political interests (Horsley 2003, 31). In light of this historical context, Nicodemus would have been aware of such an unjust practice, which is hinted at in John 7:50–51 when he stood among the Pharisees and argued on behalf of Jesus not being given a fair trial. Moreover, John 19:39–40 reports that, after the crucifixion, he came with Joseph of Arimathea (also noted as being wealthy), to retrieve Jesus' body.

What might have really resonated with Nicodemus was what Jesus was teaching. Perhaps Nicodemus was fascinated with the way that Jesus had put a "new spin" on the Mosaic Law by recognizing that Jesus Himself was the Person who would put people in touch with the Spirit of the Law and the underlying purpose of it. Jesus did so without badgering people with superficial notions of purity—notions that were often used in a way that prevented leaders from actually being able to help people. Superficial notions existed such as prohibitions against touching the dead or half-dead, even when a mere touch, along with a sincere expression of faith, might have resulted in the person's healing (see Leviticus 21). Perhaps this unfortunate circumstance had resonated with Nicodemus because he represented a wing of the Pharisees and/or temple officials who held this faulty belief.

By the time that Nicodemus went to Jesus by night, he could have possibly been fed up and desperate. Perhaps he realized that he had been born into a corrupt system, and maybe it was too far gone—both the Roman and the temple systems. He might have realized that he had been caught up in a Greco-Roman "prosperity gospel" mania that, in his day, had already gone corrupt and sour! Perhaps he realized that this dishonest system needed to be overhauled, and that the kingdom principles that the man Jesus taught represented the way in which the system would have to be overhauled.

With this in mind, maybe that is why Nicodemus asked Jesus what he would have to do to be born again—short of going back into his mother's womb, which wasn't even possible. Once he reached out to Jesus in this way, just as Ann in the introductory story gave Jesus her heart—something happened. For, in the upcoming scenes in which Nicodemus appears, the reader sees a changed man. No longer is Nicodemus sneaking around by night. He is openly challenging the temple officials, and he doesn't seem to care whether they accuse him of coming out of Galilee or of being a follower of Jesus (see John 7:50–52). Even further, he boldly prepares the body of Jesus for burial—in broad daylight (see John 19:39). Having a personal encounter with Jesus is truly a life transforming experience!

Nicodemus's image of himself had changed. Scripture carries very little information about Nicodemus beyond the gospel of John, and only a few Scriptures within this gospel tell anything about him. But, just as Ann emerged from an oppressive situation where she had once been constrained, Nicodemus had been locked into a world system that also governed his behavior. However, when "reading between the lines," all of his actions point to Nicodemus receiving his salvation. The conclusion we must draw is that salvation is available to everyone—God's salvation is extended to the rich, those with worldly goods, as well as the poor, those suffer from lack. Nicodemus and Ann are proof that we all need the Savior, Jesus Christ.

BACKGROUND RESEARCH

1. Write a short biography of Nicodemus based on Scriptures from the gospel of John (John 3:1–16; 7:37–52; 19:37–42).
2. What window into the Sanhedrin Council occurs in Acts 5:17 and 23:6–7?
3. Imagine that Nicodemus had been in the crowd, observing, when the action in the following passages from Mark and Luke took place. How might he have reacted? What questions might have entered his mind about Jesus (Mark 5:21–43; Luke 7:7–15; 8:41–55)?
4. Review the content in this chapter that has to do with the environment in which Nicodemus found himself. Then read Exodus 20. What were some of the contradictions of the Mosaic Covenant that were being violated in Nicodemus' time?
5. Imagine that there was a silent member of the crowds in the scene depicted by Mark in Mark 10:2–12, 29–30, 43–44. Given what was said about Nicodemus' possible background, if it were true, what might he have thought about what Jesus said? What about Jesus' words might have appealed to him?
6. Imagine that Nicodemus was somewhere, in the background, listening as Jesus said what He said in Mark 10:13–16. Given the environment in which he was living, and that some of the Greco-Roman practices concerning children were found being practiced by Jewish temple aristocrats, how might Nicodemus have reacted? What role might this have played in his coming to Jesus by night?
7. Project Nicodemus as a background, unnamed, and unnoticed character in the gospel of Mark, who heard what Jesus said in Mark 10:17–27. Considering Deuteronomy 24:14–15 in your analysis, how might Nicodemus have reacted to Jesus' words? How might this have figured in his willingness to ask Jesus what he could do to be born again?
8. Based on John 3:16, what does a person have to do to be saved? Can a person inherit salvation (John 1:12–13, 33)?

QUESTIONS FOR REVIEW

1. Review the introductory story. What are some factors that might have been outside of Ann's control that caused pain in her life?
2. Identify some of the places through whom God's voice spoke and through whom God reached out to Ann?

3. What are the pre- and post-salvation images of Ann? Where is Ann getting the energy to accomplish the things that she is now accomplishing?
4. What are some parallels between Ann and Nicodemus?

RECASTING THE CHARACTERS

Try to predict what is going to happen when Ann, from the introductory story, attends the family reunion.

QUESTION FOR REFLECTION

Do you feel a need for a change? Based on the content of this chapter, who is a good resource for bringing that about?

COOPERATING VS. COMPETING

Jacob and Esau: Genesis 27:34–35, 41; 33:1–4, 8–11

Aisha had moved back in with her mother and stepfather, David, just in time for the family reunion. She was sitting on her old bed, thumbing through the family albums. Each picture brought back a different memory. She had paused, carefully studying the pictures of her stepgrandmother whom she once called "Miss Pocahontas" behind her back. This grandmother had long straight black hair, beautiful olive-toned skin, high cheekbones, and had never seemed to tire of bragging about her mixed Native American, Irish, and African ancestry. She had also bragged about how her great grandparents had migrated from the South to work in the factories of the small town in which they lived, becoming property and business owners when most Black people were living in the housing projects nearby and were on public assistance.

Aisha was almost the complete opposite of this "Miss Pocahontas" in skin color and features. She still remembered, with pain, the night when, as a child, she had overheard her mother telling David, her stepfather, that Miss Pocahontas was never going to accept her mother because of the darkness of her complexion. She could still hear her mother talking through her tears that night, saying that Miss Pocahontas had always complained about her and had insinuated that she could never "measure up" to David's previous wife, who had died of cancer two years before their marriage. His previous wife had the same skin color and hair type as Miss Pocahontas.

Since the day Aisha had overheard that conversation, she had always suspected that Miss Pocahontas had favored her stepsister over her because Aisha's stepsister looked more like David's previous wife. As Aisha continued to thumb through the album, she recalled the arguments that later began to erupt between her and her sister whenever they had returned from visits to Miss Pocahontas' home. These were arguments over whether her sister had been playing into her grandmother's favoritism, and over whether her sister had a superiority complex. This antagonism between her and her sister had developed into competition over who was the prettiest, and who could get the best grades. Aisha always got the better grades, but her sister got most of the attention from the boys at their high school, where there was a very obvious male shortage.

Aisha recalled that her senior year in high school was the worst year of her life. Her stepfather, David, had lost his job because his factory moved overseas. Miss Pocahontas had died of cancer, one of several people in the neighborhood who had been diagnosed with it that year. Upon passing, she had left money for David and her stepsister, but nothing for her. She remembered walking down the main street near her home one day thinking about the toxic waste site that had been discovered not too far from there. She had passed one boarded up store after another, and had wondered whether any of them had become the sites where local drug dealers were doing their clandestine business. She had stopped to sit on the steps of the church where she had gone as a little girl. By that time, she and her family hadn't been to church in years.

She had sat there thinking about how irritated David had become since he had lost his job and how he was beginning to drink more heavily than ever before. Her parents had even separated temporarily. However, Aisha did find happiness in winning a four-year scholarship. She had applied to Fisk so that she could get away from home. Her sister had later moved to Los Angeles. After she had graduated from college, Aisha was forced to move back home with her parents until she could locate employment.

Today would be the first day that she had seen or spoken to her sister in four years. She was happy to be home and happy that they were having a reunion, but she really wasn't looking forward to interacting with her sister.

A CLOSER LOOK

Aisha and her sister have much in common with Jacob and Esau. In both cases, the wedges between them ultimately seemed to have been caused both by pressures from outside of their families and from pressures outside of their immediate relationships. In both cases, the difficulties surrounding their relationships seemed "haunted" by "ghosts" of the past. They could not see the bigger picture, which was spiritual in nature. Because they were unable to see the bigger picture, they were unable to allow that picture to affect how they interacted with each other and with their extended families.

The above story is set within a close-up shot on a relationship. If one would "zoom out" and take in the entire landscape, one could view the picture from outside of the house, from outside the immediate neighborhood, and from the global perspective. Ultimately, one could see the situation from its spiritual perspective. One could then see more clearly the forces that are evident within the story at work threatening to destroy this African American family. Recall that Aisha's father had become unemployed, and had developed a problem with alcohol. His unemployment, while felt immediately within the family, is connected to a larger societal issue. There is a nationwide tendency for many businesses to move overseas, leaving behind thousands of unemployed people who are often heads of their families. Companies have made these decisions in order to elevate their profit margins, too often with too little consideration for the devastation that it causes for the families and communities left behind.

Researchers on African American families have noted, in report after report, how unemployment creates economic conditions that are directly associated with instability within families (Hill 2003, 18). David's reaction to the loss of his job is a form of taking a retreat, or what psychologists call *retreatism*. It is widely recognized as one of the ways that people respond when they feel powerless. It is also widely recognized that such problems as unemployment and alcoholism can cause tensions between a husband and wife, and between siblings, bringing internal pressures into a family that is already feeling pressure from outside forces (13).

Recall that Aisha's neighborhood was also the location of a toxic waste site, and that an unusually high number of people had been diagnosed with cancer the year that her grandmother had passed. Researchers have found a larger percentage of toxic dump sites in neighborhoods where people of color reside that is far out of proportion to their numbers in the United States (Hill 2003, 10). This is a form of institutional racism that has also impacted Aisha's family, adding what is known as a stressor to an already stressful situation.

Recall also that Aisha had noticed stores that were boarded up in her community, and she was subsequently concerned about the presence of drug dealers. It is widely known that when entire communities are plunged into poverty, some individuals, rather than retreat, choose to become innovative by employing their God-given talents to destructive rather than life-building pursuits. Moreover, the larger picture would also be that communities of color have too often become the primary market for international drug marketers who prey on the vulnerability of those who feel blocked from legitimate means of survival. Such people are becoming rich at the expense of the underprivileged.

In addition to all of the previously mentioned pressures, Aisha's extended family seemed "haunted" by "ghosts" from the past. The "ghosts" in this case were the improper feelings about skin color that, for African Americans, dates all of the way back to slavery—to a time when African American women were quite often raped and/or forced into sexual relationships with the owners of plantations, with their sons, and/or with their male relatives. The result of this insidious activity was thousands and thousands of mixed-race children. Some of these children were brought into the homes of their wealthy fathers and eventually worked there as servants. Often they inherited money and property upon the death of the plantation owner.

After slavery, quite often lighter-skinned Blacks were given preferential treatment in terms of jobs and education, particularly throughout the South. In some cases, the Black people being given preferential treatment came to believe that they where actually "better" than darker-skinned Blacks. This has come to be called a form of *internalized racism*—a "ghost of the past" that has haunted many Black families. It has even caused some Black adults to treat some children in the same family better than others, mostly based on their sense that these children were "better" than the darker-skinned children.

In Aisha's family, this internalized racism had also drawn a wedge between her and her stepsister, causing them to compete for the boys at the local high school. Recall that Aisha also said that there were more girls than boys by the time she reached her senior year. This is consistent with the findings of researchers that have discovered that, while, at birth, there are equal numbers of boys and girls. However, as these same children grow older there is a progressive imbalance between the numbers of boys and girls in general, becoming most obvious by the time boys and girls reach senior high school. Some of this male absence is due to deaths occurring in gang violence often related to drugs, incarcerations of Black male youth, and the early dropping out of school by many boys. Of course, much of this, in turn, has been discovered to be related to factors such as high unemployment among male teenagers in particular (Hill 2003, 70).

Also recall that Aisha mentioned that her family had not been to church in years—a place where they would have been taught a different value system altogether. Attending church would have given them an opportunity to accept Jesus Christ as their personal Savior. The church is the place where they might have learned that God loves all of God's children equally. Researchers have studied African American families who have been able to do effective war against the types of negative forces that were operating against Aisha's family. They have found that people who overcome adversities are almost always involved in religious institutions, mostly churches. In fact, they have noted that the African American church is the strongest resource factor that accounts for differences in achievement among African American young people and their parents (Hill 2003, 135).

It is through studying the Word of God and prayer that they would have been able to gain the strength to face all the pressures that were being exerted upon their family. Through the power of prayer in the name of Jesus, the Holy Spirit of God would unite and guide them in spiritual warfare that would drive those "ghosts of the past" off of the premises of their house, and off their grandmother's house as well. Researchers have found a direct relationship between family stability and happiness and involvement with church (Hill 2003, 136). While the researchers may not ask about the level of personal commitment to a relationship with God, the statistics are strong enough to suggest that there must be some type of "holy hookup" with God, which makes the correlations come out "statistically significant"!

Families with a "holy hookup" have also been known to be more likely to utilize what Robert Hill, expert on African American families, has identified as the five most consistent strengths ("resiliency factors") of African American families: a strong achievement orientation, a strong work orientation, flexibility of family roles, strong kinship bonds, and a strong religious orientation (Hill 2003, 44). Moreover, whether headed by a single parent, both parents, a grandmother, or "other mother," "holy hookup" families have been shown to be happier and to remain intact. Perhaps it is because they are able to forgive one another on a regular basis and "keep on keepin' on"!

A CLOSER LOOK AT JACOB AND ESAU
Genesis 27:34–35, 41; 33:1–4, 8–11

Genesis 27:34 When Esau heard his father's words, he burst out with a loud and bitter cry and said to his father, "Bless me—me too, my father!" **35** But he said, "Your brother came deceitfully and took your blessing." **27:41** Esau held a grudge against Jacob because of the blessing his father had given him. He said to himself, "The days of mourning for my father are near; then I will kill my brother Jacob."

Genesis 33:1 Jacob looked up and there was Esau, coming with his four hundred men; so he divided the children among Leah, Rachel and the two maidservants. **2** He put the maidservants and their children in front, Leah and her children next, and Rachel and Joseph in the rear. **3** He himself went on ahead and bowed down to the ground seven times as he approached his brother. **4** But Esau ran to meet Jacob and embraced him; he threw his arms around his neck and kissed him. And they wept.

33:8 Esau asked, "What do you men by all these droves I met?" "To find favor in your eyes, my lord," he said. **9** But Esau said, "I already have plenty, my brother. Keep what you have for yourself." **10** "No, please!" said Jacob. "If I have found favor in your eyes, accept this gift from me. For to see your face is like seeing the face of God, now that you have received me favorably." **11** Please accept the present that was brought to you, for God has been gracious to me and I have all I need." And because Jacob insisted, Esau accepted it."

As noted in the introductory story, Aisha's family had much in common with Jacob and Esau. The Scripture passage for this chapter is only a "close-up" lens on a much more involved and complex relationship. Biblical scholars who have "zoomed out" to include the broader landscape have identified forces from outside their immediate and extended family that were exerting negative pressure on the family, pressures that seem to have evoked negative relationships between siblings, and between children and their parents. As in Aisha's family, some of these pressures seem to have taken the form of "ghosts of the past." There is also a similar pattern of the two families neglecting to use their most potent "resiliency factor"— collective insights that could have caused them to see their respective dilemmas through the lenses of a covenantal relationship with God.

Jacob's parents were divided in their affections toward their sons. Genesis 25:28 informs us that Isaac loved Esau and Rebekah favored Jacob. The Scripture implies that perhaps it was due to the differences in their physical makeup. Esau was a hunter with a rugged physical appearance; Isaac was fond of wild game and, therefore, favored his son Esau. Jacob, on the other hand, had a quiet nature and was more content dwelling inside the home. By Jacob's own admission, we learn that he had smooth skin (27:11) and the Bible says that Rebekah loved him (25:28). To understand this struggle, one has to examine it within the broader landscape of the economic "tug-of-war" that took place in the region (that would later be called Palestine). This struggle had been taking place since the days of Abraham and his family (Millard 1992, 35), when they left Ur of the Chaldees on the way to resettle in Canaan (see Genesis 11:31–12:5). The landscape had been shifting for a long time, from one inhabited primarily by collections of families that grew crops and herded for subsistence, into a series of nations that had been organizing these families into larger units. They were now being asked to grow crops for sale and to pay tributes. In essence, this change reduced the once independent farming families essentially into slaves, most of whom were barely existing on what was left after they paid their landlords (Ceresko 2001, 60).

The landscape had changed, and everywhere, highly organized states in Southern Mesopotamia were dominating the lives of most of the people living there. It had reached the point where roughly five percent of the population owned most of the land and wealth (Ceresko 2001, 33). This minority of the population lived in large, walled urban centers and controlled most of the surplus agricultural products that were grown by the masses of farmers (33). Ninety percent of the remaining masses were farmers, herdsmen, slave laborers or artisans such as carpenters. This had been evolving over thousands of years by the time that the ancestors of Jacob and Esau surfaced on the pages of Scripture (40), in what has been labeled as the Late Bronze Age (1500–1200 B.C.E.) (Richards 1992, 755). It was a brutal period, and nearly every region had its own king. Most people, who were not among the wealthy one to five percent, paid tribute and taxes.

However, the findings of biblical archaeologists and historians indicate that God was providing the Children of Israel with a set of rules by which they were to live, and it was these rules that would help them to survive outside of the domination of the ruthless kingdoms that surrounded them. It was these rules that would help them to create a community that, when unified and strong, had the best chance of outlasting the attempts of the Egyptians and nations, such as the Philistines, to keep them in bondage. The counterculture that God had promised to establish for them in Canaan would not have been destroyed. The Bible indicates that by the time that the story of Jacob and Esau took place, God had already begun revealing these insights. In fact, the body of collective wisdom had been gathered by the ancestors long before they were eventually written down in the form that we currently have today (Ceresko 2001, 40). It was this collective wisdom that would develop the Children of Israel into a federation of tribes consisting of an assemblage of extended families that were comprised of groups of individual households (Gottwald 1999, 120).

It appears that it was God's plan for farmers and herdsmen to cooperate rather than compete with one another. They would compliment each other so that, as weather conditions changed, they, within their community, could use their collective gifts for the betterment of the entire community. Eventually this community of people would take the form of the 12 tribes of Israel. The spiritual concepts that they were learning from God were concepts that were directly tied to their economic and political survival (Lewis 1976, 308).

One of the central concepts was the role of the firstborn and the related birthright. This was a tradition that insured, first of all, that the land and property of the family would remain within the family, clan, tribe, and ultimately within the entire community. In order to exist outside of one of the dominant empires that surrounded them, they needed such rules. It was a system that was designed to avoid the types of fights and assassinations that took place in the surrounding empires when the head of the ruling family died. Built into the methods by which property was passed along, and by which eventually debtors were protected, were strategies (such as the Year of Jubilee) for preventing too much wealth from accumulating in the hands of a few, at the expense of the broader community (see Deuteronomy 15; Leviticus 25).

Obviously, like Aisha and her family in the introductory story, Jacob and Esau's family had forgotten their history and the role that God had played in it, thereby becoming very petty and trifling in their ways. The people of God had indeed forgotten that the concept of the birthright belonging to the firstborn was an integral part of God's protective system for them (Kooy 1976, 272). Psychologists today would call this protective resources. God's system involved both economic and spiritual elements. It was the utter disrespect of Esau for this spiritual system (and related covenantal relationship with God) that created within him the ignorance that would cause him to sell his personal birthright for a bowl of soup. It was also an utter disregard for God's desire that the herdsmen and farmers cooperate in protecting an "ecosystem" that worked for all. Yet, one parent preferred one child over the other because of a personal affection that was due to such a superficial reality as the smoothness or roughness of his skin, although both symbolized the occupations that they held in the community.

This was the context in which the battle between Jacob and Esau took place.

It was competition, rather than cooperation, that also suggested the presence of "ghosts of the past" and involved the ancient struggle between herders and farmers throughout this area of the world. This competition went against God's system and was based on an idea that God had not provided enough for all. Rather, it was "every man for himself, and God for us all," an "eye for an eye, and a tooth for a tooth" and reflected a mentality that governed relationships between the people in surrounding nations. But God was calling the Children of Israel into the status of a holy nation and a royal priesthood (see Exodus 19:6; 1 Peter 2:9).

God had a plan, and wanted to see it through. So, by the grace of God, God took a bad situation and turned it around for good. Jacob and Esau did reconcile, and the reconciliation resulted in the father of the Children of Israel not being destroyed prematurely. It is because of this that we have the collection of stories that tell how, with God's guidance, the Children of Israel did evolve into a federation of tribes that did not, immediately anyway, take on the characteristics of the monarchies surrounding them. Praise be to

God who looks out for us, even when we forget our histories, and take on negative characteristics that can, if we do not repent, result in our ultimate destruction as a people.

BACKGROUND RESEARCH

1. Read Genesis 11:27; 12:9. What were Jacob and Esau's roots?
2. What promise had God made to Jacob's ancestor, Abram (Genesis 15:1–21)?
3. Read Genesis 25:19–34; 27; 28:5. What were the key episodes that had caused a split in the relationship between Jacob and Esau?
4. Using the Scripture assigned for this chapter, describe how Jacob and Esau reconciled their relationship.
5. Read Genesis 15:1–21 again. What might have been at stake?

QUESTIONS FOR REVIEW

1. What pressures from outside Aisha's family were affecting her relationships with her relatives?
2. What "ghosts of the past" haunted Aisha's family? Explain how their inability to deal with these "ghosts" created faulty thinking?
3. What was the greatest potential resource that Aisha and her family had for handling these pressures?
4. What pressures from outside the family of Jacob and Esau might have been exerting pressures on relationships between members of his family?
5. What was the greatest resource that was available to Jacob, Esau, and their family for avoiding a permanent rift in the family?

RECASTING THE CHARACTERS

1. Select the role of one of the characters in the introductory story. What is the first step that this character needs to take to see his or her situation differently? What is the next step, and so on?
2. What needs to be done to make the neighborhood in which they live more viable?
3. Pretend that the entire family has reconciled and has gone through a "healing of memories." What potential does this family have to positively impact their neighborhood and community? How?

4. What steps, educationally and spiritually, would each family member (even the stepgrandmother) need to take to be able to play their respective parts in making such an impact?
5. What role would forgiveness play?

QUESTION FOR REFLECTION

How do the points that were raised in this chapter apply to your life?

SHARING VS. DUMPING

Ruth and Naomi: Ruth 1:8–18; 4:13–16

It was Sunday evening. As usual, the family gradually gathered on Grandpa Norton's porch. Janet was in her favorite spot, in the hammock, watching over the banister as the children played "hopscotch" on the sidewalk below. Her Aunt Beverly had gone to the corner market to get some Neapolitan ice cream, her grandmother's favorite. It had been almost a year now since she had come to Detroit to live with her grandparents on her father's side of the family. She had come with what was left of the part of her family that had been living in New Orleans. A hurricane had stricken the city, and the levees near their home had broken. The streets had flooded and their home had been completely destroyed. Her great-aunt, on her mother's side, had been living in a nursing home, and, to date, they did not know what had happened to her. They were unable to get to the other side of the city in order to rescue her. However, over the past year, it seemed like small groups of family members were arriving almost every week.

It was truly a miracle how the family had come together. Her brothers had been on the police force, and one of her sisters had been in the National Guard. Somewhere, in the hurry of trying to evacuate everyone in the neighborhood, some children had been separated from their parents. The children had never found out where their parents were, but one little girl would not let go of Janet's father's hand. She clung to him and insisted that she go with him wherever he went. Janet laughed to herself as she thought about how that little girl and her brother had become a part of their family. Even though her parents already had adopted two children, and were caring for a third foster child, they made room for this child.

Her brothers had babysat with the children while she had taken a job at the corner drugstore. Her mother had gotten a job doing domestic work at the nearby hotel, while her father got a job as a security guard at night so that he could look for a higher paying job during the day. Her cousin Andrea was driving a cab until she could save money to go to beauty school. Her uncles had even assumed responsibility for cooking some meals while various adult family members were at work.

Once the ice cream arrived, her grandfather, as usual, began talking about the good old days. Today, he talked about how, when he was a little boy, his family had moved north from Tennessee, with his parents and grandparents. He told how that was a time when so many families had left the South to locate better employment, and to get away from the terrorism of the Ku Klux Klan. He told of how, at first, his mother and father had lived on the second floor of a two-story building. He told of how, as his mother's relatives had come from the South, they had all moved into the same apartment.

Then the owner had decided to sell the two-flat where they were living in order to move to the suburbs. His grandparents had saved enough money to purchase the building. Then there had been more space for other relatives who had come from the South. His grandfather had helped various relatives to get jobs at the automobile company where he had been working. As each family had additional children, they had to locate housing elsewhere. However, none of the family members moved that geographically far from one another.

Janet's grandfather talked about how everyone had to assume responsibility for doing housework, babysitting, and for loaning each other money for bus fare and food until each family had become financially stabilized. Those were the good old days, her grandfather said. Janet felt a sense of calm, as the song "God Has Smiled on Me" was still playing fresh in her memory from the morning worship service. She was looking forward to her second semester in the local university where she had been able to continue her studies for free!

A CLOSER LOOK

The circumstances that Janet's family have faced are not unusual. According to a *National Survey of Family Households*, as late as 1992, one out of three (34%) Black households have members of three generations living in the same residence (Chase-Lansdale, Brooks-Gunn, and Zamsky 1994, 380). Moreover, according to Robert Hill, renowned scholar on the African American family, among the major strengths that account for the survival of African American families are: a strong religious orientation, strong kinship bonds, a strong work orientation, adaptability of family roles, and a high achievement orientation (Hill 2003, 10). Janet's family certainly seems to be exhibiting these strengths.

Elmer Martin and Joanne Mitchell Martin, in their survey of Black extended families, found that most had representatives of more than one generation living in the same household, or often living in very close proximity. These relatives were found to depend on each other. Usually the extended family was organized around one central family member (quite often the grandmother or grandfather), who guided the family and was the link through which distant family members communicated with the local family. The Martins found this network to have a built-in mutual aid system that provided economic and psychological support. They found that seven out of nine of the central figures are women, usually between the ages of 60 and 85 (Burton 1996, 200).

One of the major strengths that come into play when facing crises such as those described in the introductory story is the willingness to adapt family roles. Hill believes that this is a strength that has passed through the generations from Africa (Hill 2003, 107). His research reveals that it was particularly useful during slavery when numerous people, sometimes from various families, lived under one roof. In such conditions, mothers sometimes performed duties that, from the perspective of European-based cultures, traditionally would have been seen as suitable only for men. Fathers, on the other hand, also had to assume responsibilities for duties that, in European-based cultures and in the more privileged culture of the Southern plantations, would have been assumed by women only. Moreover, even children had to perform parental functions on occasion, taking care of their younger siblings at very young ages, while their parents worked side by side in the fields. In this context, Black families did not have the luxury of adhering to rigidly defined gender roles. They had to do what was necessary to survive.

African American women could adapt and survive in that context due to traditions that had been passed down to them from Africa—traditions where, in famous marketplaces like those in Kumasi, Ghana, women owned businesses that helped to support their families. During slavery, Black people also had to become flexible in terms of who was defined as a parent. For example, some families had to informally adopt children who were not directly related to them biologically, because, quite often, the child's parents had been abruptly sold away from them to another plantation (Dunaway 2003, 51). However, the flexibility of parenting roles was also derived from African culture, where all of the children of a traditional village were seen as the children of the village, as well as being children of individual families (Hill 2003, 47).

Informal adoption has certainly continued beyond slavery, particularly within Black extended families. In many cases, families have established informal networks whereby they adopt children of some of their relatives who are unable to care for them. In other instances, women bring numerous foster children into their homes. Hill found that such women often allow these children to interact with their biological parents on a regular basis. Hill also found that, commonly, families did not distinguish any difference between these children and their own biological children. A common practice was for foster children to be informally adopted, without formal legal arrangements (Martin and Martin 1978, 39).

This adaptability in parenting roles has also been found to be true when it comes to how families help to care for children born to unmarried teenaged mothers. For example, Hill cites numerous studies, some of which date as far back as 1930, showing African American families being much less likely to abandon or schedule for adoption children born to teenaged mothers—children that might be considered "illegitimate" by the larger American culture (Hill 2003, 123).

Of course, most Black families have been found to prefer that their daughters and sons wait until marriage to have children. This is particularly true of parents with strong faith commitments. However, research shows that when teenage daughters do become pregnant, Black extended families are significantly more likely to assist the teenager in caring for the child than the family would be likely to release the child for adoption. Statistically, they are also significantly less likely to abandon the children than would be the case for the larger American culture. Hill cited studies showing that African American children have accounted for only 8.4% of all children in institutions for abused children (Hill 2003, 130). According to the U.S. Census Bureau, between 1970 and 1990, alone, the percentage of Black children being cared for within extended family networks grew from 1.3 to 1.6 million, bringing the overall percentage to 16%. Of these, 41% are within homes of relatives where neither of the child's biological parents is present and three-fourths are with grandparents (125). Of children in households of parents without either parent present, 80% were found informally adopted by their relatives. Only 20% have been found in institutional foster care arrangements. The formal term for this arrangement is *kinship care*. Some of these arrangements take place because the biological parents have problems with substance abuse, while some are HIV infected. Kinship care has been found to be more stable than other forms of adoption and foster care (126).

Often African American grandmothers have taken on this responsibility for numerous reasons. However, the grandmother who adapts her role to become parent of her grandchildren is also said by Hill to have roots in the strong roles that women of that age range played in African villages. This role continued to figure prominently in the Black community during slavery. There, older Black women assumed the responsibility for keeping together whatever part of the community could be kept together, even when parents were sold away from their children to other plantations (Hill 2003, 129).

Regarding Black single parents, with the psychological and spiritual support of Black extended families, many Black single parents (single for a variety of reasons) have been able to successfully raise children in large part due to help from outside of their immediate household. When single parents at the same income levels are compared, it was found that Black single-parent families (10%) are almost as likely as two-parent families (13%) to eventually have children who enroll in college. However, surveys have also shown that usually Black single-parent women who raise boys successfully have external support. Those who were surveyed said that they had sought positive male and female role models outside their families, at church, and within their extended families (Hill 2003, 129).

Counter to the negative media images of single-women-heading families, Hill found only two out of ten depended upon public assistance. In fact, since 1970, while the number of Black single-women-heading households increased from 8% to 26%, those who remained without a high school diploma decreased from 60% in 1970 to 29%. A number of famous African American men have been raised by single mothers: neurosurgeon Dr. Benjamin Carson, Rev. Jesse Jackson, and former Secretary of State Colin Powell (Hill 2003, 115).

Since 1970, the number of single Black men raising children alone has risen by 256,000. Since 1980, half of them reported being separated or divorced, one out of five widowed, and two-thirds never married. Three-quarters were found raising their biological children, while one fourth were found raising children for whom they were not the biological parent, including: nieces, nephews, or grandchildren (Hill 2003, 116).

Regarding two-parent homes, Hill cited surveys that found those who were most successful to be those who were in regular contact with extended families, and those who were willing to adapt their family roles. African American two-parent families were found sharing responsibility for economic support of their children, and sharing responsibility for household tasks (such as babysitting) involved in raising children (Hill 2003, 108).

While the Black extended family has been a major asset for the African American community, both the Martins and Robert Hill call attention to problems that can develop within this otherwise strong resource. Often problems develop when family members "dump" rather than "share" responsibilities within the network. That is, the system can break down when almost the entire burden for keeping the system operating smoothly is placed onto one person. This is particularly dangerous when the person is either too young, or is at an age where he or she cannot handle this responsibility without endangerment to personal health. "Dumping" everything on one person is psychologically unbeneficial to the person. Moreover, it is not beneficial to the family that finds itself unable to function without that person.

"Dumping" most often occurs involving the guardian of the generations, or the grandmother, on whom the burden rests. The Martins call the overburdened grandparent a "non-evolved grandmother," because she is a perpetual parent. She is the family psychologist and spiritual advisor, as well as the only person who can deal with those (mostly substance abusers) who demand an unfair share of the matriarch's and/or the extended family's collective goods and services (Boyd-Franklin 2003, 73; Martin and Martin 1978, 17).

Conversely, the situation described immediately above can also become self-abusive, when the grandmother in question will not relinquish the unfair load of responsibilities that should be shared with other members of the extended family, even though she is unable to handle it physically or psychologically. Further, abuse within the extended family network can also occur when children are burdened with responsibilities that they are not developmentally ready to handle. An example would be forcing children into a parenting role—that is, where they assume the role of caregiver for younger siblings when they are too young to be able to handle it. Such children are not likely to be able to handle the rejection that comes when they cannot meet their parents' expectations.

A CLOSER LOOK AT RUTH AND NAOMI
Ruth 1:8–18, 4:13–16 ·

Ruth 1:8 Then Naomi said to her two daughters-in-law, "Go back, each of you, to your mother's home. May the Lord show kindness to you, as you have shown to your dead and to me. **9** May the Lord grant that each of you will find rest in the home of another husband." **10** Then she kissed them and they wept aloud and said to her, "We will go back with you to your people." **11** But Naomi said, "Return home, my daughters. Why would you come with me? Am I going to have any more sons, who could become your husbands? **12** Return home, my daughters; I am too old to have another husband. Even if I thought there was still hope for me—even if I had a husband tonight and then gave birth to sons—**13** would you wait until they grew up? Would you remain unmarried for them? No, my daughters. It is more bitter for me than for you, because the Lord's hand has gone out against me.!" **14** At this they wept again. Then Orpah kissed her mother-in-law goodby, but Ruth clung to her. **15** "Look," said Naomi, "your sister-in-law is going back to her people and her gods. Go back with her." **16** But Ruth replied, "Don't urge me to leave you or to turn back from you. **17** Where you go I will go, and where you stay I will stay. Your people will be my people and your God my God. Where you die I will die, and there I will be buried. May the Lord deal with me, be it ever so severely, if anything but death separates you and me." **18** When Naomi realized that Ruth was determined to go with her, she stopped urging her.

Ruth 4:13 So Boaz took Ruth and she became his wife. Then he went to her, and the Lord enabled her to conceive, and she gave birth to a son. **14** The women said to Naomi: "Praise be to the Lord, who this day has not left you without a kinsman-redeemer. May he become famous throughout Israel! **15** He will renew your life and sustain you in your old age. For your daughter-in-law, who loves you and who is better to you than seven sons, has given him birth." **16** Then Naomi took the child, laid him in her lap and cared for him.

The story of Ruth and Naomi is certainly an illustration of the power of an extended family. It also illustrates the five strengths that Robert Hill identified in African American extended families. Similar to the family described in the introductory story, the story of Ruth and Naomi also illustrates a commitment to faith, strong family bonds, a strong work orientation, a strong achievement orientation, and the ability to adapt family roles. When the curtain rises on these strong women, what immediately catches the reader's attention is that all three are widows. The reader also notices that the two women have experienced a great deal of trauma through the loss of key family members.

Some time ago, Naomi and her family had become one of perhaps thousands of evacuees forced to relocate from the region around Bethlehem because of a famine. Later in the story the reader learns that Naomi's husband Elimelech had owned property within his tribe (see Ruth 4:3), but apparently they had to leave it behind when they left for Moab. The reader also learns that Naomi had lost her two sons. The text does not say how they died. She was soon separated from her daughter-in-law, because Orpah had decided to remain in Moab.

On the surface, the story of Naomi's family took place in a setting where they might have been just one of thousands of families that periodically became relocated due to unpredictable weather and/or military threats from surrounding nations. These nations, who were emerging into empires, had established rules to protect their spheres of influence and trade routes. Destitute people like Naomi and Ruth, who had "fallen on hard times," would have been seen as mere commodities, as potentially free or near-free labor. They would have been in danger of being merely absorbed into one of these exploitative systems, paying most of what they earned in taxes and tribute (Ceresko 2001, 35).

Because weather conditions were unpredictable, Naomi and Ruth could have become peasants in such conditions being plunged more heavily into debt and forced to sell whatever property they had and become slave laborers. Another scenario might have been that Naomi and her extended family might have been reduced to the status of day laborers, creating various products such as pottery for aristocratic elites (Ceresko 2001, 33). Moreover, if they had remained in agriculture, at any time, one of the military forces of the city-states could invade their land and seize their crops.

Scholars describe the entire area of Ruth and Naomi's story as chaotic. For some time, thousands of people had been migrating from place to place, searching for alternatives to the exploitative arrangements of the city-states. They fled from heavily populated and fertile areas to less populated, less fertile areas, which demanded much more work and cooperation among families in order to survive outside of the mainstream city-states. Many had tried various arrangements to avoid being subject to the rules of the city-states that were emerging into empires in the region, but had failed (Joffrey 1995, 281).

However, Naomi had come from a people that had evolved an alternative way of living together—a federation of tribes that consisted of collections of very well-organized extended families. God had given them the insights to establish the laws that governed these arrangements and to bring valuable principles into the center of their lives. Such laws helped Naomi to identify resources that she could negotiate within her *mishpaha*, or clan/family, to ensure protection for herself and her future generations (Gottwald 1999, 237). A *mishpaha* is the Hebrew word for family. However, it is used in a wider sense than the family as we know it. Consequently, the family of Naomi's time most often consisted of a larger group of relatives with strong blood ties. The mishpaha employed a system that governed who could marry whom and was designed to keep land within the families. This provided them a necessary defense from the exploitative city-states that would have reduced them all to slavery (Numbers 36:1–12).

Like the family of Janet, in the introductory story, Naomi's family was one based on long-established rules of mutual aid and generosity (Genesis 18:1–21). These rules as well as their covenant with God gave meaning to and governed their everyday alternative lifestyle. This set of rules helped them to live in the margins, outside of the confines of the exploitative city-states (Ceresko 2001, 48). They helped them to set up a type of community where several extended families collectively bartered agricultural products and pastured flocks. In these settings, there were small industries for creating pottery, tools, and other essentials. Disputes were handled by heads of families (102).

The law of the Goel, or kinsman, came into play for Naomi when she had to reposition herself within the extended family in Bethlehem, from which she once had to flee (Gottwald 1999, 237). The focus was on the preservation of land within the extended family. In this case, the role of the Goel was assumed by her husband's relative, Boaz. The Goel could redeem land (Leviticus 25:23–28), purchase back land if it had been sold, and could also buy it in advance. He could also redeem those family members who were in debt (vv. 35–55). The Goel could even redeem a poor family member who was to be sold into slavery because of debt. Moreover, the Goel was a protector who would avenge murder (Numbers 35), and was primarily responsible for seeing to it that there were male heirs (Deuteronomy 25:5–10).

While not everyone among the Israelites supported these traditions, these laws kept the community together and protected it during the time that Ruth and Naomi lived. One might conclude that the women of this story were intelligent, creative, and able to negotiate with what they had to get what they needed. They were women of faith, vision, and obedience to the covenant that the people had made with God. They recognized the potential strengths within their extended family, and found a way to make those resources work for them and for their community, even though they encountered adversity and overcame it with God's guiding hand (see Ruth 4).

BACKGROUND RESEARCH

1. What was the role of the kinsman-redeemer as described in Ruth? What did Boaz have to do before he could assume that role for Ruth (Ruth 3–4)?
2. What role did kinship play in the distribution of land (Numbers 1; 26)?
3. What later became Israel's system of land tenure (36:1–12)?
4. How was land distributed to individual families (Judges 21:24)?
5. Compare and contrast the following extended families with those that

Robert Hill and Martin and Martin describe among African Americans: Joshua 7:17; Judges 6:11, 27, 30; 8:20; 18:14, 19, 28.

6. How was property passed down from one generation to another (Deuteronomy 25:5)?

7. In your opinion, in addition to basic morality, what role might certain prohibitions against various kinship patterns have had in keeping property within the family (Leviticus 18:6–18; 20:11–14, 19–21)?

QUESTIONS FOR REVIEW

1. Name some ways in which the laws discussed in this chapter served as a protection for the extended families, clans, and tribes that comprised the early federation of Israelites?

2. What traditions, passed down to Janet's family, served as a protection in times of unexpected change?

3. In your opinion, what relationship might there be between the rules that governed the early collections of extended families in Israel and the traditions that assisted in the survival of African American families? Use your imagination.

4. Compare and contrast Janet's experiences in the introductory story with those of her grandfather.

5. Compare and contrast the experiences of Janet's family with that of Ruth and Naomi. How are they similar? How are they different?

RECASTING THE CHARACTERS

Rewrite the introductory story by inserting your family. Create a family crisis in which a family member needs help from the entire family. How might your family organize itself to address this situation? What insights would you seek from God? What insights might already be available to you in the Bible? With what resources (time, talent, money, space) has God already blessed your family? How can they be organized for the good of the entire group?

QUESTION FOR REFLECTION

Is your family a center for spiritual healing and support? What such resources are available to your immediate and extended family? In many families, these resources don't come into play in situations other than funerals. How can your extended family use its spiritual resources in creative, consistent, and nurturing ways?

FAITH "AT CENTER" VS. FAITH "OFF-CENTER"

Hannah: 1 Samuel 1:1–28

Stanford was sitting in the second row, in a pew to the right of the pulpit. The choir was singing "How I Got Over," and it was just before his brother would stand in the pulpit and preach. Resting his arm on the pew behind his wife, he drew her closer to him, glancing down the row at his children, who were now in their teens. His eyes then scanned around the sanctuary. Almost the entire Jackson family was present for this momentous occasion—his brother David's 20th year pastor's anniversary. He thought of how proud his mother would have been of David and of the entire family.

Stanford's mind traveled back to the day, nearly half a century ago, when he had gone with his mother to talk with a pastor in a little storefront church around the corner from where they had been living. He remembered how frightened he had been. He was the oldest of eight children. His mother had admitted his father into the hospital for the third time that year. She was very unsure of how she was going to take care of their children. Reflecting back on it, as he sat in the church that day, Stanford remembered how his mother had said that she really didn't want the rest of her family or any of her friends to know about their problems. He remembered how the situation sometimes seemed to cause his mother to become ill.

Due to his father's illness, his father had lost his job at the factory and they had been depending on public assistance to survive. He remembered that they had, at one time, been living in a large house in a neighborhood across town, but that their family hadn't owned that house. When they could no longer pay the rent on such a large home, the family had been asked to move. They had to look for a house where they could pay less rent. Stanford remembered how he and his brothers and sisters had to change schools and find new friends in their new neighborhood. He remembered how he and his brothers had been tempted to run drugs for a local drug dealer in order to help support the family.

That is exactly what he would have done, in fact, if it had not been for the conversation with the pastor in the storefront church that day. Over the course of a week, the pastor had invited his mother, his brothers, and his sisters all to accept Christ as their personal Savior. He remembered the pastor telling his mother that she needed to leave her children in the hands of the Lord. They began to attend church every Sunday. Stanford recalled how the people of the church invited his brothers and sisters to begin to participate in children's activities. He recalled how he and his brothers had formed a quartet, and had joined an organization similar to a Rites of Passage program. His sisters and his mother joined the choir and began attending Wednesday night prayer services. The pastor and the pastor's secretary had soon helped his mother to process the forms so that the family could receive veteran's benefits, since his father was a disabled veteran of World War II.

Amazingly enough, by the time of his brothers' anniversary that day, most of his brothers and sisters had been leaders in churches and in the community for decades. His brother, David, was a pastor. One of his brothers was a professional Christian musician. That brother's daughters had formed a trio that sang Christian music. One even had a Christian radio program. One sister had been a union steward on her job and had helped hundreds of people throughout her community. Stanford, in fact, was a statewide superintendent for Christian Education in the denomination to which his family belonged and had been serving as a superintendent of Sunday School for over 20 years. His children were also church musicians. His oldest sister had become a writer of Christian literature that was by then circulating throughout the world.

A CLOSER LOOK

Both Stanford and Samuel, God's prophet, priest, and judge (1 Samuel 1:1–28), have mothers who found themselves in seemingly overwhelming circumstances. In both situations, the mothers brought their problems to God. In both cases, they placed their children and their relationship with God at the center of their lives. Both mothers devoted their children to the Lord. They recognized that their respective religious institutions were their most valuable resources, and, in both situations, the outcomes were nothing short of miraculous!

Perhaps these mothers are not alone in their act of committing their children to the Lord. The results of a wide variety of research support the notion that Black churches have a very positive impact on young people who are actively involved in them. For example, research has shown that families having children with strong achievement orientations are families that also teach their children strong moral values—values that are also reinforced in African American churches (Haight 2002, 19). Most researchers rarely ask parents or young people whether they have a personal relationship with God. They rarely ask whether a person has actually accepted Jesus Christ as his or her personal Savior. Nor do such studies typically try to detect the strength of a given person's faith or commitment to God.

However, there are a number of studies that show a statistically strong relationship between church involvement of young people and a wide range of positive behaviors. For example, some have shown young people who consistently attend church also regularly attend school more than those who do not attend church. They have been found to be more productive than those who do not attend church, and they have been found to engage in more positive social activities. Benson and Donahue have shown that such students also have lower instances of substance abuse (Benson and Donahue 1989, 125).

Andrew Billingsley's research lends support to this idea. He found that institutions can have either a positive or a negative impact on how individuals within a given family relate to each other (Billingsley 1992, 25). It has been found that African American families are most likely to interact with the church over any other nongovernmental community institution (19). Moreover, another expert on the Black family, Robert Hill, lists a strong religious orientation as one of the chief traits that accounts for resilience and strong achievement orientations in Black young people and their parents. He cites, in particular, research showing that single mothers who raise boys with high achievement orientations typically expose their sons to role models in positive community institutions such as churches (Hill 2003, 45).

While some researchers have focused on how high achievement relates to church involvement, others have focused on whether the values taught in high achieving Black families and those in African American churches are parallel. In terms of those taught in families, Royce and Turner, for example, found that Black parents, with high achieving children (regardless of income level), most commonly taught their children how to respect themselves, "how to be happy," and how to cooperate within the family. Such families were also found teaching their children how to resist stress-producing factors in their environments and how to identify and utilize different "protective mechanisms" in their families, schools, and churches. Such parents were also found combating negative risks for their children either by reducing the risk or reducing their children's exposure to it. They were also found teaching their children various skills that could result in their overall sense of empowerment. Such values have also been found to be taught in church-based youth programs (Royce and Turner 1980, 407).

Robin Jarrett surveyed low-income parents, in particular, to discover what "community bridge patterns" parents used to help their children reach toward high goals. She discovered such adults cooperating and networking amongst themselves, collectively monitoring their children's behaviors, and mutually sponsoring youth development programs. Quite often, these networks are established through churches (Jarrett 1995, 111).

Moreover, a number of researchers have found a strong positive achievement orientation among children in families where Black parents teach African cultural values such as recognizing that opposites can exist together in harmony. This is reflected in the common African American statement, "God is good all the time!" (Hill 2003, 53). Parents at all income levels who have high achieving children were also found teaching them that they have within them what is necessary to overcome adversity—that is, "We are more than conquerors through Him who loved us" (Romans 8:37). Parents with high achieving children were also shown helping them to build high self-esteem and self-control. These parents were also found teaching their children ideologies and theologies that helped them to deal with racism. They were also found teaching them to be proud of the achievements of Africans and African Americans (Johnson et al. 2000, 9). These are also values that are taught in Rites of Passage programs and African-centered youth programs in local churches (Speller 2005, 6).

The most common practice among African American churches was providing young people with the opportunity to accept Jesus Christ as their personal Savior, which often involved an about-face in change of behavior, and a commitment to God (Haight 2002, 102). Moreover, Hill cited a number of community programs, quite a few of which partner with Black churches in providing the opportunity for young people to acquire their General Educational Development (GED) certificates. Others have been found taking young people on college tours, and assisting them with completing the applications for college, along with providing them with scholarships. Some churches have been found either by themselves or in partnership with community programs offering youth employment programs and teaching young people entrepreneurial skills (Hill 2003, 145).

Afrocentric educational programs, Rites of Passage programs, and annual Kwanzaa celebrations, in local churches, have taught young people about their African heritage, and how to deal with central challenges of being a Black man or woman in America (Speller 2005, 6). Nationwide surveys of Black churches have also found them offering parenting classes for teen parents that focus on the roles of both mother and father (Hill 2003, 117).

In a wide variety of studies, Black churches who have such programs have been shown to be "resource factors" for parents and children. They have been considered to be in partnership with the parents, who include their children. Black churches have also been shown to offer "protective factors," through after school programs that take children off the streets and away from negative influences such as gangs, drugs, and guns (Hill 2003, 135). Black churches have also been considered a place of support where parents can network with each other to provide resources for children. Hill lists a variety of programs that have partnered with families and Black churches to build kinship bonds through special adoption services, foster programs, and big brother/big sister programs (99). Moreover, a study by an organization called Public Private Ventures showed that youth who were a part of the big brothers and sisters programs had lower rates of substance abuse, fewer school absences, and higher grades in general (Tierney, Grossman, and Resch 1995, 22).

Lincoln and Mamiya, in a survey of 2,500 churches in mainline Black denominations, found a wide variety of "quality of life" programs, including preschool programs, daycare programs, nurseries, family counseling, remedial education, employment training, and recreational activities (Lincoln and Mamiya 1990, 309). Some churches have even founded orphanages, and senior citizen centers (Smith 2004, 1). Hill also cited a wide variety of outreach programs in local churches that have addressed social justice issues related to affordable housing and the revitalization of neighborhoods (Hill 2003, 135).

The above traits have made African American churches strong resource factors for a number of Black families, particularly for single-parent families. However, there are a number of issues that will need to be addressed by Black churches if they are going to be able to serve as protectors and resources for a wider variety of families. One of the issues is classism, which occurs when the socioeconomic and educational levels of the church members is much different from those of the people in the community surrounding the church. This sometimes happens when families that once had the same general background as the people in the community at one time, have reached a different income level and have moved to a different neighborhood, but who continue to commute to the same church. If the church refuses to develop programs for community children and families, the church establishes a "class" distinction between itself and the community. This behavior prevents the church from serving as a resource factor for the many families in the neighborhood who want their children to become involved in the church. However, such parents may hesitate to do so, due to their perception of "classist" and "elitist" attitudes that the church members may have.

If the church is to be a resource of role models particularly for boys and girls who do not have fathers in their homes, the apparent relatively low numbers of Black men in churches is a source of concern. In fact, there is a definite imbalance between the numbers of women and men in African American churches. After a survey of churches in mainline Black denominations, Lincoln and Mamiya found that only three out of ten members were men (Lincoln and Mamiya 1990, 304). At an overnight retreat, Jawanza Kunjufu, founder of African American Images, asked 75 Black men to tell their reasons for not attending church. They cited a wide variety of reasons, including characteristics related to the ministers, church members, sermons, and the church in general. On the other hand, Kunjufu found that in churches with African-centered educational programs and special programs of interest to men, the percentage of men in the membership is much higher (Kunjufu 1994, 25).

There is also a need for strong role models for girls—role models that illustrate how young women can continue to develop in the tradition of the strong Black women who helped to rebuild the African community after slavery. This tradition is related to the tradition of determined Black women who are currently doing their part to revitalize and build communities throughout the continent of Africa. However, one challenge facing Black churches is that many of them hesitate to allow women to use their talents, education, and skills in leadership roles within the church. This is unfortunate, because as opportunities for Black women have opened, many have pursued educational goals and have gained skills through in-service training on their jobs. These skills could be invaluable for building the types of programs that would be resources and protective factors for Black families. Unfortunately, many churches still have either explicit or implicit policies that restrict the use of these skills in building church programs (Lincoln and Mamiya 1990, 274).

Further, this is an example of poor stewardship of talent. While quite often women "make their mark" in institutions outside of the church by establishing programs with potential value for Black families, these same women have the ability to develop similar programs within churches but too often are prevented from doing so. This is so, in many cases, even though women constitute as much as 70% of the population of many local churches (Lincoln and Mamiya 1990, 274).

Of course, one of the greatest challenges facing African American churches in general and African American families in particular, is the task of preparing young people for their future roles in the struggle on behalf of African peoples on the continent of Africa and throughout the diaspora. This is a critical concern, given the degree of problems that are now ravaging communities of color throughout the world, but particularly those of African descent.

This problem is reflected in media coverage of crises facing Black Africans on the continent of Africa. Millions of Africans have lost their lives in the civil wars such as those occurring in the Sudan and Rwanda. Famines in Chad and Niger have been threatening the lives of thousands of adults and an estimated 800,000 children. Moreover, the AIDS pandemic and diseases such as malaria and polio continue to cause a decline in life expectancy. Added to all of this is the crisis of far too many African countries being held in bondage by owing enormous debts to foreign countries (Birchett and Godfrey 2005, 6).

The historical roots and levels of complexity of the previously described devastations indicate that it will require generations of struggle to even begin to change these situations. The challenge involves educational, psychological, and spiritual factors. First of all, there is the reality that large numbers of African American children, youth, and young adults have a minimal understanding and personal connection to Africa. African American educational, psychological, and social science researchers have been documenting this crisis over the past decade (Meredith 2005, 344).

Researchers Baldwin and Bell actually developed a test instrument called the African Self-Consciousness Scale, with 42 questions that measure student "competencies" such as an awareness of: one's identity, heritage, customs, and values that affirm the lives of people of African descent. The scale also detected participation in movements toward the liberation of African peoples and recognition of racial oppression. Test results summarize their ratings of agreement or disagreement with various statements such as: "I have difficulty identifying with the culture of African people" (Morris 2003, 255).

Studies based on this Likert-type scale have reported a wide spread in performances of African American college students on the test. However, a number of studies have shown that the stronger one's consciousness of being committed to Africa and African culture, the higher one's academic performance and the greater one's ability to deal with such pressures as being considered a minority in a predominantly White college environment (Morris 2003, 255). Psychologist Na'im Akbar goes so far as to argue that Black or African identity should not be considered a developmental reaction to social oppression alone, but should be considered a core personality trait that is essential for a healthy sense of internal self-integration or wholeness (Akbar 1989, 2).

Perhaps the greatest challenge facing African American parents and churches today is how to raise Black children who will become leaders and community builders of African descent at home and abroad. These are the children who will also keep spiritual values and the church at the center of African American communities.

Most child psychologists would say that the time to assist children with their sense of identity is in their formative years (even during the first five years of life), and that such assistance should continue through adolescent years. This may be the best time to begin laying the foundation for future healthy Black families and communities unified by common value systems.

A CLOSER LOOK AT HANNAH
1 Samuel 1:9–20

1 Samuel 1:9 Once when they had finished eating and drinking in Shiloh, Hannah stood up. Now Eli the priest was sitting on a chair by the doorpost of the Lord's temple. 10 In bitterness of soul Hannah wept much and prayed to the Lord. 11 And she made a vow, saying, "O Lord Almighty, if you will only look upon your servant's misery and remember me, and not forget your servant but give her a son, then I will give him to the Lord for all the days of his life, and no razor will ever be used on his head. 12 As she kept on praying to the Lord, Eli observed her mouth. 13 Hannah was praying in her heart, and her lips were moving but her voice was not heard. Eli thought she was drunk 14 and said to her, "How long will you keep on getting drunk? Get rid of your wine." 15 "Not so, my lord," Hannah replied, "I am a woman who is deeply troubled. I have not been drinking wine or beer; I was pouring out my soul to the Lord. 16 Do not take your servant for a wicked woman; I have been praying here out of my great anguish and grief." 17 Eli answered, "Go in peace, and may the God of Israel grant you what you have asked of him." 18 She said, "May your servant find favor in your eyes." Then she went here way and ate something, and her face was no longer downcast. 19 Early the next morning they arose and worshiped before the Lord and then went back to their home at Ramah. Elkanah lay with Hannah his wife, and the Lord remembered her. 20 So in the course of time Hannah conceived and gave birth to a son. She named him Samuel, saying, "Because I asked the Lord for him." (See also 1 Samuel 1:1–8; 21–28.)

It appears that Hannah, in the Scripture text, is faced with a similar challenge of leadership. In stories preceding the episodes described in this passage, the leadership of Eli's sons is already questionable. Eli's challenge was to raise a future leader that will restore adherence to center the covenant of Yahweh and to refocus Israel's attention on God. All of this is taking place parallel to the struggle within Hannah's family (see 1 Samuel 1:3).

One of the strongest images of Hannah is of her kneeling in the house of the Lord, with only her lips moving. Another equally provocative image is of her dedicating her son Samuel to the Lord. These images of Hannah, alongside the images of her husband Elkanah going back and forth to the Lord's house and making sacrifices, underscore the important role that their relationships with God played in their family life. In fact, Hannah's promise to raise Samuel as a Nazirite (see Numbers 6:1–27), appears to link her exact style of motherhood to part of the Mosaic covenant—a covenant that, throughout the stories of the Children of Israel, serves as a binding force undergirding their social, political, and economic lives as a community (see Genesis 6:18).

Scholars such as Norman Gottwald and Anthony Ceresko describe settings such as the one in which the story of Hannah occurs, as a tribal league. Such leagues are believed to have consisted of collections of clans of extended families. Hannah's story takes place within one of these extended families (Ceresko 2001, 108).

Like African American mothers, who have historically brought their children to church so that they could develop a particular value system, Hannah dedicated Samuel as a Nazirite, so that he would be taught an alternative value system contrary to those popular in the Ancient Near East. She also seemed fully aware that Samuel would be groomed for leadership growing up in the temple.

Gottwald and Ceresko provide data concerning the role of the covenant with Yahweh at every level of organization of the tribal league. This is reflected in the story of Hannah. Gottwald found such individual extended families (mishpaha) trying to be obedient to their part of Israel's covenant with God—a covenant that provided them with specific resource factors and a related value system. These protections typically included much more legal and economic security than families would have had within the empires emerging in the Ancient Near East at the time of the story of Hannah (Ceresko 2001, 48). For example, it is obvious that Hannah's extended family story occurred in a setting where extended families offered mutual aid and generosity (Genesis 18:1–21), and it is where the house of the Lord was a place for the transmission of specific values to young people (see Deuteronomy 6:7).

It is also a setting where the mishpaha (clan/large extended family) held yearly feasts and pilgrimages (see 1 Samuel 1:3). These families might have included those who possibly no longer lived within a specific originating household (vv. 4–5). Gottwald speculates that, in the case of Hannah, the extended family itself might have had at its center an established holy place where their annual family feasts took place (Gottwald 1999, 282). This would be similar to the way in which Kwanzaa is practiced in African American communities today.

In many Bible stories, there are images of the covenant that are central to the life of the league, the individual tribes, the clans, and of any given extended family (mishpaha) within the clans (see Joshua 3:3). By the time of the setting of the story of Hannah, the people of Israel believed that Yahweh was guiding them in their struggle to create a new type of community. The Bible describes how the Israelites responded to the call of God to be a holy nation and a royal priesthood (see Exodus 19:5–6). This charge brings with it a set of values for living in community. Gottwald and Ceresko believe that such values would have had to do with being liberated from the oppressive empires that were quickly emerging around them— empires that were looking for slaves and people to put into debt bondage. The covenant of God with Israel stated concerns for social justice— particularly as it related to the weak and vulnerable (see Leviticus 25:13–17).

In Hannah's time, the covenant with Yahweh was a defining feature of Israel—one that distinguished it from the surrounding nations. Each person was seen linked to God, linked with the covenant, and linked with his or her family—whether individually, collectively, or tribally, as in collections of extended families. Rather than God working through a few elites, as the city gods of the Canaanites are described, Israel's God, Yahweh, is seen working with and through an entire people by transforming them and giving them an alternative life style.

That is the mission of which Hannah wanted her son to be a part. Hannah appeared to see her maternal role as a part of a holy community-building process. In that sense, Hannah reflects every mother who brings her child to a church-based educational program—programs which, in partnership with parents, are designed to produce spiritually inspired leaders for the African American community and for the world.

BACKGROUND RESEARCH

1. Read Numbers 6:1–27. List specific value systems that were built into the preparation of the Nazirites.
2. Read the following Scriptures: Genesis 16:2; 30:1–23; 1 Samuel 1:6, 27;

Isaiah 47:9; 49:21. How do these Scriptures depict barren women being treated?
3. Read 1 Samuel 1:12–17. What was the crisis of leadership that was facing Israel?
4. Read 1 Samuel 8:4–22. Make a list of traits of the heads of some of the empires that are reflected in this story as surrounding Israel at the time.
5. Read 1 Samuel 3:1–11. Under what circumstances does Samuel become aware that God is calling him to a special task?

QUESTIONS FOR REVIEW

1. What are some differences and similarities between Hannah and Stanford's mother in the introductory story?
2. What are some differences and similarities between Samuel and any one of the people named in the introductory story?
3. "Reading between the lines," make a list of values that the church might have transmitted to any one of the characters in the introductory story.
4. In what sense does Stanford's mother "partner" with God in raising her children?
5. Name some specific ways that Hannah can be said to be an image with whom African American women have related.
6. In what ways did the church serve as a resource in these stories?
7. In what ways did the church serve as protection?

RECASTING THE CHARACTERS

Write Scene II of the introductory story. In the scene you write, create a scenario where any one or group of family members in the story begins to prepare the next generation to work on behalf of Africa and Africans throughout the world? What would the steps be? Where would you begin? What role would the church play? Build all of this into Scene II.

QUESTION FOR REFLECTION

What resources are available in your local church? How can you and/or your family use them to create a stronger family that is spiritually motivated toward high achievement?

UNITING VS. FRAGMENTING

Shadrach, Meshach, and Abednego: Daniel 3:1, 4–6, 16–23, 26–28

It was Sunday night. Some members of the Marshall family were gathering in the living room as others were straightening up the dining room, and still others were working in the kitchen. Over dinner, Mr. Marshall had just introduced the idea of a family stewardship project. While each family member was already paying individual tithes to their local church, Mr. Marshall felt that it would be good if the family, collectively, could locate a project, perhaps in Africa, that it could support, above and beyond the personal tithes that each individual gave to their local church.

God had really blessed the family, Mr. Marshall had said. Each member, other than their youngest daughter (who was in elementary school), had a job. Mr. Marshall was now the head of his department at work, and had received several substantial raises over the past few years. Mrs. Marshall had just completed her second masters degree, and was being considered for a position of assistant principal at the middle school where she taught. They were still talking about the idea of the stewardship project, as Michael, the oldest son, was putting the last of the dishes into the dishwasher. The family then slowly gathered in the living room as the 9:00 evening news feature program came on the cable station that they were watching.

Surprisingly enough, it was about a crisis that was taking place in a remote area in central Africa. A reporter was interviewing four young men who had escaped from refugee camps there, had been caught, and had been put into slavery, but had escaped. Miraculously, they had traveled all of the way to the United States. It seemed like an interesting story to Michael, who planned to research it further for his high school senior essay.

It wasn't long before the entire family had gathered around the television set.

"At least a million people have been chased from their homes into refugee camps," one young man told the reporter.

"I remember how my family used to take turns sleeping at night," a second young man said. "We always had to have one person who remained awake, to look out for the militia group that had been raiding villages and burning them to the ground."

"One night the government even bombed the village where we lived," said a third young man. "All I remember is that it looked like fire that was raining down from the sky."

They told the story of how, one day, when the four brothers had gone to the well to get water for the rest of the family, suddenly a ghostly looking man from an extremist Muslim group descended upon them with rifles and took them into slavery. The man would not call them by their original African names, but gave them new Arabic names.

The four boys were from Christian families, but the Sharia law that was governing that area of their state would not allow them to take a Sabbath rest on Sunday, as they had been accustomed to doing. These Islamic fundamentalists would not allow them to attend church, and had threatened them that if they did not give up their religion, sooner or later they would be killed for violating one of the Sharia laws. However, the four brothers told the story of how they had banded together and had made an escape.

The young men told the story of how they successfully fled from slavery but had to wander around Africa for years—through Ethiopia, to the Sudan, and back through refugee camps in Kenya.

"The militia that had been raiding our villages shot at us when they discovered that we were escaping, but we ran," the first young man told the reporter.

"If it had not been for the Lord on our side," another young man said, "we would have been destroyed."

The news feature ended with the reporter saying that two million people had died and four million were now sitting in refugee camps as this civil war continued to rage. For those roughly 3,600 that the United States government had allowed to immigrate to the United States, they had been separated into groups of threes and fours and sent to cities throughout the country.

"One of the things I really appreciate," said one of them, "is that now I can have my real name back. I don't have to keep answering to a foreign name, and I can attend church freely. It took a long time and it was frightening, but God was with us all the way."

Mrs. Marshall turned off the television set, and asked that the family take a moment of silence and then pray that God would lead them in making a decision about how they could use some of the resources with which God had so richly blessed them to in some way help African families who were in crisis. Jackie, the oldest daughter, volunteered to research the Internet and their church denomination to locate some nongovernmental organizations working in Africa that the Marshall family might decide to support (Sawatzky 2005).

A CLOSER LOOK

The four young men from Africa, in the introductory story, are not unusual. In fact, 3,600 such young men recently entered the United States as refugees, and are known in the popular media as the "Lost Boys of Sudan" (Goffe 2004). However, what is striking about them and so many others in similar situations is their heroic struggle to remain faithful to God, and to keep whatever is left of their families together, regardless of the forces that are determined to fragment them. What is also striking is that some have been bonding together and creating "fictive kin." Fictive kin is a term that refers to people who are not related through birth or marriage, but who share a significant emotional relationship with someone, taking on the characteristics of a familial relationship. Therefore, the young men featured in this chapter were determined to keep some of the spiritual and psychological benefits of extended African families alive, doing so with people who are not actually their blood relatives.

This story is a close-up perspective on the particular predicament of these four young men. However, if the camera lens were to "scope back," it would take in a panoramic view of economic and political realities that have roots that go all the way back to the period of colonialism in Africa. Around the midpoint of the 20th century, when so many African countries gained independence, in some parts of Africa chaos also ensued. This resulted in civil wars and waves of migration where, in some cases, entire communities were displaced and chased into refugee camps within and between countries. In some countries, this activity has taken place over a period of decades (Meredith 2005, 344).

In the latter part of the century, in many communities throughout Africa, Africans could be seen fleeing Arab extremists who were taking over the governments of African countries and enforcing the Sharia laws. Included in these laws were the changing of names, the enforcing of the Arabic language, and the outlawing of Christianity and traditional African religions. Moreover, the Sharia laws enforced very stiff penalties including executions and dismemberment of body parts for disobeying them. Issues over these laws have provoked many civil wars. The "Lost Boys of Sudan" have been documented in the media as fleeing this type of "bigger picture" of political and economic reality (Bixler 2005, 6). However, the good news is that these young men have testified repeatedly that God is not dead! They testify of what they consider to be daily miracles of resistance, survival, and victory.

There is great potential for American families, particularly African extended families and churches, to do whatever they can to help families that are affected by these realities. Families all over the world are still being dismantled due to war and famine. Further, families are regularly being abducted into slavery. The State Department of the United States government has been publishing an annual report on countries that are still illegally abducting large numbers of Africans into slavery, both within and from outside of given countries' borders (U.S. Department of State 2005, 25).

It has been estimated that at least forty-five million people worldwide are homeless. These unfortunate people are either wandering around as refugees from one country to another, or wandering around within the borders of their own countries. Moreover, in Africa, alone, the HIV/AIDS virus has killed parents of some fifteen million children. It has also been estimated that so many people have died from AIDS in Africa that in some countries, the life expectancy figures have been reduced by at least half. In other impoverished African countries, children are dying on a regular basis due to illnesses that rarely kill children in wealthier countries (Carruthers, Haynes III, and Wright Jr. 2005, 15).

In some parts of Africa, millions of people are being killed by people of different ethnic groups and/or races. This is what has been technically termed *genocide* and it is another force that has been dismantling African families. Most families being displaced from their homes and forced into refugee camps are women and children. Moreover, in many cases, child soldiers are being recruited and armed with heavy machine guns. Such wars have been raging for quite some time in Burundi, the Ivory Coast, the Democratic Republic of the Congo, Uganda, the Sudan, Somalia, Sierra Leone, Liberia, Eritrea, Ethiopia, Angola, the Central African Republic, the Republic of the Congo, Mozambique, and Mauritania (Riverside 2005, 1).

In some refugee camps, women and girls are being raped on a daily basis. In African countries, women who are raped are stigmatized in addition to suffering from the long-term effects of the rapes. In these same centers, reporters have said that there have been so many killings that people have been buried in mass graves. Moreover, these situations are being made much more serious by current and impending famine (Hoge 2005).

Remarkably, news programs that have covered these conflicts have quite frequently noted how people are either trying to keep the fragments of their families together and/or are creating new families among "fictive kin." Also encouraging is that more and more African American churches and families have been joining hands with African families to demonstrate that God still loves them. Such families have recognized the importance of being willing to become expressions of God's love in the lives of other families in need (Hill 2003, 135).

More exciting news is that so many families, caught in these circumstances, refuse to give up on God! In many ways, it is just one more way in which they have been talking back to the empires worldwide that have been negatively impacting their lives by neglecting them.

A CLOSER LOOK AT SHADRACH, MESHACH, AND ABEDNEGO
Daniel 3:1, 4–6, 16–23, 26–28

Daniel 3:1 King Nebuchadnezzar made an image of gold, ninety feet high and nine feet wide, and set it up on the plain of Dura in the province of Babylon.

3:4 Then the herald loudly proclaimed, "This is what you are commanded to do, O peoples, nations and men of every language: **5** As soon as you hear the sound of the horn, flute, zither, lyre, harp, pipes and all kinds of music, you must fall down and worship the image of gold that King Nebuchadnezzar has set up. **6** Whoever does not fall down and worship will immediately be thrown into a blazing furnace.

3:16 Shadrach, Meshach and Abednego replied to the king, "O Nebuchadnezzar, we do not need to defend ourselves before you in this matter. **17** If we are thrown into the blazing furnace, the God we serve is able to save us from it, and he will rescue us from your hand, O king. **18** But even if he does not, we want you to know, O king, that we will not serve your gods or worship the image of gold you have set up." **19** Then Nebuchadnezzar was furious with Shadrach, Meshach and Abednego, and his attitude toward them changed. He ordered the furnace heated seven times hotter than usual **20** and commanded some of the strongest soldiers in his army to tie up Shadrach, Meshach and Abednego and throw them into the blazing furnace. **21** So these men, wearing their robes, trousers, turbans and other clothes, were bound and thrown into the blazing furnace. **22** The king's command was so urgent and the furnace so hot that the flames of the fire killed the soldiers who took up Shadrach, Meshach and Abednego, **23** and these three men, firmly tied, fell into the blazing furnace.

3:26 Nebuchadnezzar then approached the opening of the blazing furnace and shouted, "Shadrach, Meshach and Abednego, servants of the Most High God, come out! Come here! So Shadrach, Meshach and Abednego came out of the fire, **27** and the satraps, prefects, governors and royal advisers crowded around them. They saw that the fire had not harmed their bodies, nor was a hair of their heads singed; their robes were not scorched, and there was no smell of fire on them. **28** Then Nebuchadnezzar said, "Praise be to the God of Shadrach, Meshach and Abednego, who has sent his angel and rescued his servants! They trusted in him and defied the king's command and were willing to give up their lives rather than serve or worship any God except their own God.

The biblical story of the Hebrew boys—Shadrach, Meshach, and Abednego—takes place in a background that is very similar to that of the "Lost Boys of Sudan." The story occurred within the context of the Babylonian Exile, and it is the Babylonian Empire that had taken them into slavery. As is the case of the Sudanese boys, this story happened during a time of war and exile. It unfolded as King Nebuchadnezzar besieged Jerusalem (see Daniel 1:1). Eventually most of the aristocracy and government officials were banished, leaving behind only a remnant of the people. When the curtain rises on Shadrach, Meshach, and Abednego, the king had ordered that some of the best specimens from among the exiles be brought before him for civil service. The king called for members of Israel's royalty and nobility. He wanted handsome young men without physical defects (v. 4).

One of the first things that the king did was to change their names from those related to God (Hananiah, Mishael, and Azaria), to those related to the Babylonian gods (Bel, Marduk, and Nabu). Then he attempted to take away their religion. When they resisted, he "stepped up the heat" and put them in a fiery furnace! However, the young men still would not worship the king's god or change their devotion to the God of Israel.

Similar to the "Lost Boys of Sudan," the pressure on these young men, in slavery, was tremendous. However, the Hebrew boys maintained their faith in God and banded together as "family." In the end, even the king had to take a second look at their God (see Daniel 3:28). Their families appear to have been victims of what has come to be called the Babylonian Exile. Along with thousands of others, they were forced out of their homeland when King Nebuchadnezzar of Babylon besieged Jerusalem (see Daniel 1:1). In the process, many people were separated from their families. Similar to the situation of the "Lost Boys of Sudan," these biblical people were among millions that were banished from their homeland Judah. The Scripture shows them as being impacted by international economic and political forces that created an even greater issue with which God's people had to contend.

As in the circumstances of the "Lost Boys of Sudan," by the time that the curtain rose on the young Hebrew boys, their homeland had been devastated. The entire economy within Judah had collapsed. The population had been significantly reduced and large numbers of those left behind were perishing due to disease and starvation (Smith 2004, 77). This happened as Nebuchadnezzar, in three waves of deportations (597, 587, and 582 B.C.E.), removed most of the members of the royal families, the nobility, the civil servants, the priests, the people who kept the temple, the merchants, the artisans, and craftsmen. What remained in Judah were the poorest artisans, peasants, shepherds, and only lower ranking officials (see Jeremiah 52:24–27).

By the end of the exile, the majority of Jewish people lived outside Judah, and Jerusalem had become mostly a symbolic religious center. In many countries, they were living in isolated and abandoned areas that already needed rebuilding and redevelopment. Many of those who were living in Judah existed as poor farmers and landless peasants on large estates that had been left vacant by banished landlords. Yet, even these families maintained their village and family networks based on cooperation and mutual support. This would become the foundation from which the future Jewish community would be built again (Ceresko 2001, 41).

One of the primary sources of strength for these exiled people was their memory of God's goodness to them. They saw God as a life-giving force (Isaiah 41:17–18; 55:1–2), as a source for food (Isaiah 49:9–10), and as a source of guidance (Isaiah 42:16; 51:3; 55:10–11). Moreover, in their thoughts about Jerusalem, they spoke in kinship terms (Isaiah 49:18–20, 22) (Clifford 1976, 490).

BACKGROUND RESEARCH

1. What is the setting for the story of Shadrach, Meshach, and Abednego (Daniel 1:1–2)?
2. How did the King of Babylon want to use Shadrach and his companions (vv. 3–5)?
3. At what point were the Jews taken into captivity (2 Chronicles 36:7; Daniel 1:1)?
4. What were the original names of the young men (v. 6)?
5. In your opinion, why might the king have changed the young men's names (Genesis 41:45; 2 Kings 24:17)?
6. What is one image of God that the Israelites continued to hold, even in captivity (Isaiah 41:17–18; 55:1–2)? What is another (Isaiah 49:9–10)? What is yet another (Isaiah 42:16; 49:19, 21, 51:3; 55:10–11)?

QUESTIONS FOR REVIEW

1. What are some differences and similarities between the "Lost Boys of Sudan" and Shadrach, Meshach, and Abednego in the Scripture passage for this chapter?
2. What is the "bigger picture" surrounding the "Lost Boys of Sudan" mentioned in the introductory story?
3. What is the implied "bigger picture" surrounding Shadrach and his companions?
4. Explain some ways that the "Lost Boys of Sudan" have resisted the attempts of their enemies to destroy them.
5. Explain some ways that the young men in Daniel 1 resisted attempts of their enemies to destroy them.

RECASTING THE CHARACTERS

Select a character from within the Marshall family in the introductory story. Then write Scene II of the drama from the perspective of that character. Be sure to show that character contributing to the family project of locating and supporting one or more nongovernmental organizations working out of Africa.

QUESTION FOR REFLECTION

In what ways might the content of this chapter relate to your life and/or the lives of your family members, both immediate and extended?

INVESTING VS. WASTING

The Widow at the Temple: Mark 12:38–44

It was one of those lazy Sunday afternoons and, as usual, Jennifer was lying on the couch in her mother's living room and watching television while her mother and her mother's friends from church were having dinner in the dining room, just behind her.

As she lay there, with her mind fading in and out of the women's conversations, she remembered how things had been unfolding since her father had died. Nearly every Sunday, for the past two years, she would leave her apartment, drive over to her mother's house to pick her up, and then drop her off at church. Then her routine was to drive over to her favorite breakfast brunch, do a little shopping, pick up a *New York Times*, and gradually head back over to the church where she would meet her mother and her mother's friends and drive them over to her mother's house.

She would then take up her position on the couch and either watch television or read the newspaper. Each of the six women were widows. Each had a different story to tell.

Over the past two years, the women in this circle had heard her mother's story many times. Jennifer's mother had described the day that the doctors discovered that her husband had lung cancer and that he had less than four months to live. She talked about how the Women's Fellowship had come to see about her and how the deacons, the pastor, and her family had been at her side when her husband had made his transition. She told them about how grateful she was that the prayer circle had invited her to be a part of it. Throughout the past two years, it was common for Jennifer's mother to share funny stories about various episodes in her life as she had tried to get her finances in order and how difficult this was. Her husband used to handle their financial matters. She never even thought that she would need a driver's license.

Over the past two years, Sister Allen had also shared her story many times. She was raising three of her grandchildren because her daughter Marva was not able to do so. Marva was addicted to crack cocaine. Nearly every other week, the women in this circle had heard a different episode from Marva's life. She had once been involved with a man who was also addicted to crack. In fact, Marva was not sure whether this man was the father of one of her children. He was now in prison for robbing a local grocery store. However, Marva was still living a dangerous life and was frequently arrested by the police. Sister Allen didn't really trust her daughter, but she had taken the children in order to keep them from being placed in foster care.

Sister Fredericks, another member of the circle, was caring for her son's children. He had custody of his two teenaged boys from his previous marriage. They stayed with Sister Fredericks while her son worked and supported them. However, her son's job was in another state. The boys had been getting out of hand, violating the rules regarding curfew that their grandmother had set. Sister Fredericks felt that they needed to stay with their father, but she thought that she was the only one who was available to care for them.

Sister Atchison was somewhat younger than the other women in the circle. Her husband had been killed by accident in a gang shoot-out. Sister Atchison's daughter, Donna, had become pregnant as a teenager. However, Donna was too young to locate the type of job that would pay enough for her to be able to afford her own apartment. Therefore, she lived with her mother until she could get a high school diploma and a job. Sister Atchison's stories always had to do with differences between her and Donna over how to raise the child. She wanted her daughter to live with her until she could support herself. However, she had to work during the day, and she was always worried that Donna might be getting together with the father of the child, and that she might end up becoming pregnant again.

Sister Meeks, another woman in the circle, was also taking on the role of a mother again. Her husband had died almost 20 years ago, and she had just retired from the post office. The children of her best friend Victoria had come to live with her because Victoria had just been diagnosed with breast cancer. The chemotherapy treatments had been leaving her completely exhausted. Originally, Victoria had adopted these children, but she did not feel that she was going to be able to take care of them for long. Her stories were always funny, as she shared about the differences between raising her own children and the children that she now had in her custody.

However, of all the women in the circle, Sister Anderson lived in the most dangerous neighborhood. She would get up and walk her two nieces and one nephew to elementary school every morning and pick them up in the afternoon. However, she was always concerned that she might be robbed, because there were numerous crack houses within the two block radius surrounding her home. She didn't want any of the crack dealers or gang members to try to recruit her nephew to sell drugs or join a gang. She had developed arthritis in her lower back and was beginning to have trouble walking.

Sister Anderson had confided in the women of the circle that she was not sure whether she could get any public assistance to meet some of the children's needs. All she had was her Social Security benefits, and that wasn't enough to purchase all of the clothing they needed, school supplies, food, and other necessities. She had shared with the women that she was worried about her sister, the grandmother of the children she was keeping. Her sister had become an alcoholic, due to some of the stress of becoming a mother again at 55 years of age. Her sister had given up her seniority and pension on her job in order to take care of her grandchildren.

However, on this particular Sunday, the women were talking about how much they missed Sister Reynolds. Sister Reynolds had been 72 years old. She too had become a mother again when her great-granddaughter Cherise had become pregnant as a teenager. Her granddaughter Mary, her great-granddaughter Cherise, and Cherise's baby were all living with her, and she had been trying to help support them. Mary wasn't working but was dependent on public assistance. Sister Reynolds and Mary would combine their incomes in order to see that everyone had somewhere to live. However, Sister Reynolds had recently found out that she had a very aggressive form of cancer, and, within four months' time since it was detected, she had passed on.

As Jennifer lay there, listening to these remembrances and stories, she thought about how they, and the other people from their church, would always greet each other with, "Praise the Lord, Sister or Brother...." She also thought about the fact that over the past 30 years, her mother had belonged to the church and had been tithing 10% of her income to God through the church. She had overheard the other women saying that they had done likewise. When she asked her mother about this, her mother said that they were not giving it to the church, but were being obedient to God by supporting the programs of the church so that God could help others through the church. *That is remarkable*, Jennifer thought, as she got ready to take her nap.

A CLOSER LOOK

The widows in the introductory story, on many levels, seem to have "made a way out of no way." That is, on one level, they have formed a sense of family among friends, or "fictive kin" (those people who are not blood relatives, but have chosen to develop family-like relationships with one another) in situations where they might otherwise have been lonely and isolated. Their "fictive kin" seem to be both the women in the circle and the people of the local church. On another level, the women have formed families within families (or extended families) where what had been the "nuclear family" (mother, father, children) had broken down. On yet another level, the women demonstrated their willingness to be flexible in their roles within families, recasting their roles of grandparents into the role of parent again—an ability that Robert Hill, expert on African American families, says is a major strength of Black families (Hill 2003, 107).

In terms of being a grandparent, scholars who have studied the African American family have noted that the strong, African American grandmother has a rich history that extends all the way back to Africa. It extends to the villages where older African women in extended families had great authority over other members (particularly women and children) in the family complexes and villages (Hill 2003, 47). During slavery, quite often older Black women, who had reached the age where they were no longer physically strong, were less likely to be traded to other plantations than younger women. Infants and children in early childhood were also unlikely to be traded, at least for a time. However, their parents might have been traded to other plantations. Therefore, the grandmother, or the older Black woman, on the plantation quite often had the responsibility for caring for such children, without the help of a husband, who also might have been traded to another plantation (Dunaway 2003, 150).

The role of the strong Black matriarch in the extended Black family continued after slavery. Elmer and Joanne Martin, experts on the Black family, found that seven out of nine dominant family figures were women who had outlived their husbands by as many as 18–30 years. This was particularly true when the husband's early death had been caused by overwork, causing him to die before retirement and receiving benefits that would have supported the widow (Martin and Martin 1978, 17). Strong Black matriarchs have been responsible for keeping the generations together, and quite often have been in charge of the household that became the center of the Black extended family. It is even common for several generations to live in the one household of the Black grandmothers (Taylor, Chatters, and Jackson 1993, 332). It has been estimated that one out of every three Black households consists of three generations, and that at least 1.3 million to 1.6 million Black children live in multigenerational households, that is 13–16% (Hill 2003, 123). Of course, such strong central figures have also been surrogate, or voluntary parents, who have not necessarily been the biological grandmother. This includes aunts, uncles, godparents, and fictive kin (129).

Traditionally, the strong Black grandmother has been held in very high esteem in the Black extended family. More often than not, she has also been the spiritual center of the family, passing on the traditions, and encouraging both her children and grandchildren to remain in church. Often she has assumed the responsibility for bringing children to church when their immediate parents fail to do so on a regular basis. Experts on the Black extended family have cited research that underscores the important role that Black grandmothers have played in being just the "cushion" that a single parent might need in order to be able to make a new start by gaining the resources that would allow him or her to independently care for his or her family (Chase-Lansdale, Brooks-Gunn, and Zamsky 1994, 374).

However, experts on the Black family have also warned that too much can be expected of this strong Black matriarch by other members of the extended family. Assuming that this one person is strong enough to ultimately bear all of the extended family's problems, some members of the family may tend to unfairly "dump" too much responsibility onto them, placing their health and financial security in jeopardy. In some cases, it is only after this person has passed on that irresponsible members of families suddenly discover that they can locate other resources to help them raise their children, help them get free of drug addiction, and help them locate employment (Minkler, Roe, and Price 1972, 752).

When the kindness of the strong Black matriarch of the family is being taken advantage of, the entire family system can become dysfunctional, with people in the family system not being willing to share the load of responsibility for taking care of family members who need the help from the entire extended family (Boyd-Franklin 2003, 73).

As mentioned above, this is important to explore, considering the rising numbers of African American women who are both widows and grandparents, and who are now responsible for completely raising either their grandchildren or their great-grandchildren. While a considerable number of African American grandparents are as young as 40 years of age and even younger, still, most widows are 60 years of age and older. Studies have shown that older African American widows are likely to have far fewer resources than younger single parents and younger widows (Chase-Lansdale, Brooks-Gunn, and Zamsky 1994, 373).

African Americans comprise only 6% of all Americans 60 years or older. Only 40% of that number (6%) are African American men. That means that 60% of the African American population over 60 years of age are women. Moreover, according to the 2000 Bureau of the Census Report, ten percent of all African American women are widowed, compared to three percent of Black men. A recent report, *Profile of the Black Elderly*, by Alexander Harper, shows that the majority of African American women 65 years of age or older (57.7%) are widowed, and Black women are tending to become widowed earlier than White women (Harper 1991, 21). That is, most African American women between the ages of 60–85, in most cases, have outlived their husbands (Cox 2002, 7).

Other studies are showing that older single/widowed African American women's lives are being made more complex due to the stresses associated with finding it necessary to raise children at such later stages of their lives (Burton 1992, 744). For example, there has been a dramatic overall nationwide increase in the number of grandparents and other relatives who are assuming responsibility for raising grandchildren, having increased by at least 44% since 1980. Today, there are at least 3.7 million grandparents who are raising grandchildren. Of those, the majority (2.3 million) are grandmothers (Cox 2002, 2). Exact percentages vary by community and region of the country. In New York City alone, for example, estimates are that at least 12% of all children are being raised by grandparents (2).

For Black children, the percentages also vary. The 2000 U.S. Census reports show that, nationwide, at least 12% of Black children are in the care of grandparents (most of whom are more than likely Black women who are either single and/or widowed). A similar survey of Head Start students in predominantly Black areas in Oakland, California, showed that as many as 20% of the children who are enrolled live with grandparents. In a predominantly Black Oakland junior high school, more than half of the 750 students were living with grandparents. In a Northwestern urban community, 30% of children enrolled at a particular elementary school were found being raised by grandparents (Burton 1992, 746). One study found that out of 664 African American families, 45% of mothers between the ages of 19 and 26 were living with their mothers (Chase-Lansdale, Brooks-Gunn, and Zamsky 1994, 379). A number of surveys of Black grandparents found them ranging mostly between the ages of 44–85 (Cox 2002, 2).

However, the traditional reasons for African American grandparents assuming responsibility for their grandchildren have changed over the years. At one time, the arrangement was mostly temporary. For example, some grandparents kept grandchildren while parents migrated North to find employment and then sent for their children. Another scenario was that a teenager would become pregnant and her mother would keep her and the children until she was able to complete high school, even college in some cases, get employment, and then assume full responsibility for her children. Moreover, some grandparents were actually only part-time parents who agreed to shelter grandchildren for parts of the year from hazards of northern city life, for example, by keeping them in the South during the summers (Cox 2002, 7).

However, today, a number of nationwide surveys have found the primary reasons for grandparents raising their grandchildren are: drug addiction of the children's parents, HIV/AIDS, mental illness of one parent or the other, and imprisonment of the parent(s). Moreover, quite often the grandparent is raising the grandchildren at the same time he or she is either caring for one or more elderly parents (68%), caring for other elderly relatives (15%), and at the same time worrying about the "ups and downs" of their own children (parents of the grandchildren), they are caring for and watching them go in and out of drug rehabilitation or prison, or declining physically with the onset and advancement of AIDS (Cox 2002, 2).

Another persistent source of stress is the fact that often such grandparents do not have enough money to handle the responsibilities they have assumed. One survey found 57% of them describing their financial status as "barely getting by" (Burton 1992, 747). The same survey found 67% of those surveyed unemployed, and of those, as many as 20% being dependent on Social Security. One study found the majority of grandparents surveyed to be retired, with an average annual income of $13,500, and with some still being dependent on Social Security benefits. In some cases, such grandmothers reported having been forced to leave their employment and lose their pensions due to the emergency nature of the situation that made it necessary for them to immediately become parents again (Cox 2002, 7).

Other sources of stress have to do with the environments in which some grandparents and widows are raising grandchildren. Many grandmothers and widows live alone with their grandchildren. When they are living in high-crime urban areas, where there is known to be heavy drug traffic, periodic drive-by shootings, and burglaries, they are under even more stress. Such dangerous conditions outside the home have been found to dictate their daily and weekly schedules. Some surveys show as high as 86% reporting feeling "depressed or anxious," with one survey showing 36% of those surveyed reporting that they are drinking heavily and developing new medical problems. Some, in fact, have been found to be in physical conditions that are too serious for them to be taking care of young children, children with special needs, or rebellious teenagers (Cox 2002, 7). Quite often the situation is aggravated by the fact that some widows have to deal with anxiety and depression while trying to process grief related to the loss of their husbands (2).

Amazingly, in spite of all of this, so many African American women in such circumstances have not forgotten God, but, rather, they cling closely to God. Research on the Black church by Lincoln and Mamiya, for example, revealed that, in a large percentage of the churches of mainline denominations that were surveyed, women comprise as high as 80% or more of the congregations (Lincoln and Mamiya 1990, 304). Moreover, any observation of such congregations would reveal the high percentage of older women who are both widows and grandmothers. Because most churches are financed by tithes and offerings, it is remarkable that these very women are still finding a way to allow their funds to make a major contribution to the financing of the operations of their churches through their tithes and offerings.

It is also amazing that so many of these same women are responsible for creating the support systems within churches that help people to "get over" in times of crisis. So often they are the ones who prepare people for baptism, as well as sing the songs that so many people embrace as they "walk the aisles." After their work for the Lord is done, they must then walk out of the church and face the oftentimes rough circumstances that they will encounter throughout the week. It is these courageous women who populate the weekly prayer meetings, teach Church School, and collect the money that goes toward creating scholarships for young people who are going away to school. Moreover, many have worked even outside of the church buildings, in various civic organizations in projects that develop Black communities. Most members of Black churches and families can testify that, truly, these women have given all that they have of their time, talent, and income to build the Black community, Black family, and the Black church.

It is no surprise that today, so many African American churches are exploring and instituting ministries, organizations, and programs that can provide help to African American grandparents, particularly widows, in perhaps their current and greatest hour of need.

A CLOSER LOOK AT THE WIDOW AT THE TEMPLE
Mark 12:38–44

Mark 12:38 As he taught, Jesus said, "Watch out for the teachers of the law. They like to walk around in flowing robes and be greeted in the marketplaces, **39** and have the most important seats in the synagogues and the places of honor at banquets. **40** They devour widows' houses and for a show make lengthy prayers. Such men will

> be punished most severely." 41 Jesus sat down opposite the place where the offerings were put and watched the crowd putting their money into the temple treasury. Many rich people threw in large amounts. 42 But a poor widow came and put in two very small copper coins, worth only a fraction of a penny. 43 Calling his disciples to him, Jesus said, "I tell you the truth, this poor widow has put more into the treasury than all the others. 44 They all gave out of their wealth; but she, out of her poverty, put in everything—all she had to live on."

The widow in this passage has in common with the widows in the introductory story that she, too, was willing to give all that she had to support what was designated as the spiritual center of the community. By all indications, she is undoubtedly in the middle of a very difficult and challenging situation. Like many of the women in the introductory story, she found herself trying to survive in a hostile environment with very few resources. By all indications, she faced general cultural prejudices, financial pressures, and a political environment that was on its way toward exploding.

Regarding prejudice in Jewish tradition, widowhood was sometimes treated almost like a curse. Widows were considered cursed because their husbands' deaths were possibly premature. Premature deaths were seen as a calamity brought on by God's judgment (see Ruth 1:20–21; Isaiah 54:4). The widow was viewed as guilty by having been associated with the husband who had experienced an early death. This tradition is further implied in the term *widow*, which in Hebrew means "mute." That is, perhaps the widow was expected to be silent in disgrace. It is also possible that widows wore special garments to identify their status as widows.

The term *widow* itself was used as a metaphor for a less than equal state of affairs. For example, the book of Isaiah uses the term to describe the upcoming state of Babylon (see Isaiah 47:9), which was expected to lose its population and become destitute, like a widow. The author of Lamentations 1 and 5 used it to describe the current state of Israel, by describing a widow being plunged into poverty and servitude (Lamentations 1:1; 5:3–4).

Mark 12:38–44 makes it clear that this widow was poor. Her two small copper coins (mites) would have been equivalent to 1/64 of a laborer's daily wage. It doesn't appear that she was covered by the Levitical laws that provided various means whereby widows could reenter families and become part of the lines of inheritances. If she had been from among the Levites, for example, and if she had been childless, she could have returned to her father's house to await a marriage, even if it meant "marrying" someone who was much too young to be a husband in any real sense (see Genesis 38:11; Leviticus 22:13; Ruth 1:8–13).

Considering the context in which she surfaces on the pages of Scripture, her status seems ambiguous. However, it is within the context of Jesus' criticisms of the scribes' treatment of widows (see Mark 12:38–40). It therefore raises the question of whether she once had property but lost it due to some unfair treatment or scribal interpretation of the law. In terms of faith, the passage shows her standing in stark contrast to the scribes. If one were to put this short story into the foreground, against a backdrop of the story of the sower scattering seeds on various types of ground (see Mark 4:1–20), it would appear that the scribes are perfect candidates for being considered the hard, rocky ground, whereas this poor woman is an excellent candidate for one who would have responded as though the seed was falling on her good ground. Jesus admired her for her faith.

However, there are other indications that the widow of this passage might have been very vulnerable, living in a very insecure and potentially hostile environment. "Reading between the lines" of the Hebrew Bible, there appears to have been a negative tradition whereby widows were taken advantage of by others. This situation might have provoked the prophets into speaking out against that type of oppression (see Isaiah 1:23; 10:2; Malachi 3:5). However, God has the last word for making God's love for widows known. That is one of the reasons that there were specific directions in the Jewish laws about how to treat widows (see Deuteronomy 14:29; 24:17, 19–21; 26:12; 27:19). Such directions are also found in the New Testament (see Acts 6:1–6; Luke 20:47; James 1:27).

The widow in this passage was obviously a very courageous woman. There are a number of unanswered questions that add to her mystique. She appears to be surrounded by people who had much more money than she. Was she from the peasant class—one who had fallen on hard times, due to a famine, or due to debt bondage? At the time, there were many more peasants than aristocrats, and, collectively, it was funds from the peasants that supported the temple and the government (Horsley 2003, 105). Moreover, it was the funds of peasants in places surrounding Jerusalem and in Galilee that paid major tribute in taxes to the Roman Empire—funds without which the empire would have collapsed.

Richard Horsley and other scholars have described the mid-first century environment in which this woman would have lived as one of ongoing political strife and military conflict. An oppressively high level of taxes (as much as 30–60% or more) of income from products was exacted from the peasants in order to fund the massive building projects and to sustain the rich lifestyles of aristocrats and government officials (Ehrman 2004, 241; Goodman 1997, 146; Freyne 1980, 155; Jeremias 1969, 58).

Apparently a series of famines and drought frequently caused peasant farmers (perhaps the class from which the widow in this passage came) to be unable to produce crops at their usual level. In such a case, they might not have been able to pay both the temple and the government taxes, and subsequently might have lost their property. Seizing such property was one of the ways that aristocrats were able to build wealth (Horsley 2003, 15). Angry peasants, facing these conditions, conducted revolts. During the time of Jesus' ministry and during the time that this woman would have been living, these revolts would have been growing, and there would have been numerous precursors to organized Jerusalem terrorists later known as the *Sicarii* (39). This dangerous Jerusalem environment would have been the one in which the widow found in Mark 12:38–44 would have been living.

Consistent with most of the women who surface on the pages of the gospel of Mark, this woman is an example of one who had great faith. In spite of the circumstances that have her in poverty, and the stresses that are no doubt associated with it, she still makes the trip to the temple to honor what she considers is the right thing to do (Malachi 3:10). She has in common with the widows mentioned earlier in this chapter that she gives her all, depending only on the promises of God. Perhaps it is for this reason that she catches the attention of Jesus. God, through the writer of Mark, included her as an example of great faith. In addition to being among those whose money helped to sustain the temple in Jerusalem, she has been an inspiration to countless numbers of widows throughout time. Women of faith, such as these, have done what they could, through contributions of time, talent, and resources, to sustain hundreds and thousands of churches, as spiritual focal points of their communities.

BACKGROUND RESEARCH

1. What is one interpretation of widowhood that might have affected how people in first century Palestine saw the widow from today's passage (Ruth 1:20–21; Isaiah 54:4)?
2. How might people have been able to identify widows (Deuteronomy 24:17)?
3. What comparisons are drawn between Babylon and widows (Isaiah 47:9)? What comparisons are drawn between Israel and widows (Lamentations 1:1; 5:3–4)?
4. Consider your answers to the previous question. What insights do these Scriptures give you into the types of lives that widows in Israel might have lived?
5. What do the words of prophets reveal about how widows might have been treated (Isaiah 1:23; 10:1–2; Malachi 3:5)?
6. What provisions were written into the Law for widows (Deuteronomy 14:28–29; 26:12–13; 27:19)?
7. What evidence is there from scriptural passages that widows in first century Palestine might have required special consideration of the community (Luke 20:47; James 1:27)?
8. What might have been the primary reason that the widow brought her coins to the temple (Malachi 3:10)?
9. What instructions and promises does God have for the widow (Jeremiah 49:11; Psalm 146:9)?
10. What is one basis of the women in the introductory story greeting each other with the words, "Praise the Lord, Sister or Brother!" (Psalm 68:4–5)?

QUESTIONS FOR REVIEW

1. Review the introductory story. In what sense is the support group that these widows have created a "family" or "fictive kin"?
2. What words of Jesus can be applied to the "family" that the women have created (Matthew 12:46–50)? Explain in detail.
3. As the introductory story stands, what seems to be missing from the stories being told by these widows?
4. If each of these six women have belonged to the same church for 30 years, and if each one earned an average of $12,000 per year, and if each one contributed 10% in tithes, taken together, how much would this group of women have contributed to the upkeep of the spiritual center of

their communities? Multiply this amount by the number of such widows that might be located in your local church.

5. Are there any widows in your church, community, or family who are in circumstances similar to those described in the introductory story? What are some ways that your family, church, or community could assist them in this ministry in which they are involved?

6. Create a list of needs that the women in the introductory story have in common, and those that are unique to them as individuals.

7. Considering your answer to the previous question, design a church-based support program for widows and grandparents raising grandchildren. What needs would it address, and how?

RECASTING THE CHARACTERS

1. Consider Jennifer, the daughter in the introductory story. Write a Scene II for her. Might God be calling her to do something? If so, what? Build that into the scene.

2. Select one of the widows in the introductory story. Write Scene II for her, incorporating her family into helping her with the responsibility of raising the grandchildren. More than one family member can be involved.

3. Design a church-based support system for widows and grandparents raising grandchildren and great-grandchildren. Be detailed. What services could be provided? How?

QUESTION FOR REFLECTION

Are there ways in which faithful widows have touched your life? How can you follow their examples? How can you give back?

RITES OF PASSAGE
(RESPECTING VS. DISRESPECTING)

Jesus and His Earthly Parents: Luke 2:41–52

It was Friday night, and the men and boys of Second Baptist Church were gathered around the campfire at their annual Rites of Passage Retreat. It was an event that had been long-awaited and greatly anticipated. By the end of this weekend, most of the boys would be moving up one age grade. Several others would actually be formally inducted into manhood. Brother Franklin, the director of the program, glanced over the group as the boys sat around the fire roasting hot dogs. It had been a long year, and he could tell, by the looks on their faces, that they were proud of what they had accomplished. The boys of the church had been meeting with the men of the church for the past year, twice a month.

The boys had been organized by age levels, and each age level had been given the name of a different African country. Within each group, they had learned so much about the Bible, about African and African American history, and about how to make good use of educational opportunities at church and school. These resources would prepare them to assume their future roles within the African American community and the world. On this particular weekend, they would each make a more formal commitment to the principles that they had learned, and each would get a chance, once again, to make a renewed commitment to the Lord.

At this particular opening ceremony, each person would get a chance to share what the Rites of Passage program had meant in his life so far. Brother Franklin listened closely as the testimony session began. Sitting directly across from him were three brothers who originally had been brought by their foster parents to the Rites of Passage program.

As Steven, the oldest of the brothers, began to speak, he told of how he had been in foster care for as long as he could remember. He hadn't seen his real parents for years. He and his brothers had been taken away from their parents and, so far, no one had adopted them. He told of how he had been transferred from one school to another and from one foster home to another, until he had come across a family from this church. He told of how he had never had any men in his life to whom he could relate.

Steven continued to talk about how he had never learned, anywhere, the things that he had learned in this program. Most of all, he said, he felt that he now had a personal relationship with the Lord and with the people in the program. In fact, he felt like the group to which he had been assigned was like a family to him. He said that, whereas he did not have a family before, now he felt that he belonged in God's family, and he had decided to devote his life to serving Jesus Christ.

Then Darien told his story. Darien had just gotten out of the juvenile detention center two years ago. He had been detained after being arrested for armed robbery. He was only 13 years old at the time. Before that, he had run away from home, and had somehow made his way from Detroit to Chicago. Eventually he had run out of money and had found himself homeless, wandering from one shelter to another. He had begun breaking and entering into people's homes and cars, and robbing people on the street whenever he could, just to have money for food and transportation. He had been reported to the police numerous times, but on the day he was finally arrested, he was trying to rob a store with a gun that he had brought with him from Detroit.

It was in the juvenile detention center that he had met Brother Franklin and the men of the prison ministry of Second Baptist Church. They had opened up a branch of the Rites of Passage program at the center and a number of boys there had joined. "It became one of the brightest moments of my week," Darien explained. He talked about how he thought it was so natural to come to the church after he got out of the detention center, and how the church had helped him to locate employment and to acquire his high school diploma. He said that the church had become family to him, and he told of how he would never forget what the church had done.

Patrick then told his story. At first he didn't want to join another church organization. He was already in the choir and had been serving on the Junior Usher Board. But his grandmother had insisted that he join this group. He had no idea that it was going to be as much fun as it was, and he was glad that he had come. He had accepted Christ as his Savior when he was in elementary school, but this program had really helped to make the Bible come alive. In fact, he had never known about the Black people in the Bible.

Then Anthony told his story. His family had come to Chicago from Haiti, and he had been new to the neighborhood at the time that his parents brought him to Second Baptist Church. They had soon after enrolled him into the Rites of Passage program. His accent was different from that of the other children at school and some of them were cruel to him. He had even been beaten up several times by a bully in the elementary school that he attended.

When Anthony's parents brought him to the church, everything changed. Anthony met new friends. He talked about how much he had learned about his African heritage, something that he soon realized he had in common with African Americans. The men in the group also allowed him to share things about his home country. He felt that they appreciated him and thought he had special gifts to offer the group.

Then Rodney shared his testimony. He felt that he had been called to the ministry, but he had been afraid to tell anyone, because he had thought it would make his life miserable. He was already known to be a "nerd," because he liked to study, and he was already laughed at by some of the people at his school because they always saw him with books. He was also known as the "preacher's kid."

However, he had learned, in this group, that he did not have to prove anything to anyone, and he did not have to feel unusual because he liked to study. In fact, through this group, he had learned that liking to study was a gift from God. He thanked the group for making him feel comfortable with his call to the ministry, and for being there for him as he made preparations to go away to college in the coming year.

Other boys shared about how they had been going to church all their lives, but that they had never really had things explained in the way they were presented in this group. In fact, they were happy to be able to participate in making decisions about so many of the group's activities. They said they felt that they had some say in what was happening to them for the first time in their lives.

Then one of the fathers shared. Brother Singleton, who had enrolled two of his sons into the program, shared how it was all a matter of obedience. He had his Bible with him, and he read from it how Moses had told the Israelites to pass down the traditions and God's teachings to the next generation. What better tradition than to tell the story of how God had brought African Americans through the wilderness of slavery, he said. He felt that he was being obedient as a parent, and he was so glad to see the fruit of his obedience.

Another one of the men, who worked with the program, joined in with Brother Singleton, saying that at first he didn't want to take time away from his profession to spend it with young people. However, he had heard a sermon one Sunday and felt that God was speaking directly to him. He felt that he had so much to thank God for, and that it was only right to obey God and share his wisdom and experience with the boys at his church as they made their way toward manhood.

Brother Franklin was so moved by these testimonies. He could tell, by the responses of the other men who had come to the retreat, that this was going to be a great weekend.

A CLOSER LOOK

Feelings of abandonment, alienation, and being lost and being found are powerful themes that run through many of the above testimonies. On the other hand, themes that are just as powerful are those of faith, obedience, formation of family, and formation of community. The stories contain images of the African American church at its best. They contain images of the wide range of differences among the people who are being blessed by it. They also contain images of the power of committing one's life to Jesus Christ. These boys' stories are a part of the overall story of what can happen in the Black church—an institution that has roots extending back through slavery and into Africa. The Black church has stood at the center of the Black community, with arms wide open, whether it has been as the "invisible institution" in the "hush harbors" in the "wee" hours of the mornings during slavery, whether it has been as the spiritual center of the community during the Jim Crow era and segregation, whether it has been the storefront that welcomed those who were migrating North to get away from the Ku Klux Klan and to seek jobs, or whether it has been as a beacon of light at the center of what is sometimes modern urban chaos. It has been a center where African Americans from many different backgrounds have connected with God. Rites of Passage programs are just one more expression of this tradition.

However, the previous story reflects that perhaps one of the primary groups now in need of the spiritual development services of Black churches are young African American males. These are the young people who are living in a variety of what has previously been considered nontraditional living arrangements. The 2002 U.S. Census indicates that people under the age of 18 now comprise about 33% of the African American population. In addition, the 2002 U.S. Census reports that a larger proportion of Black males than non-Hispanic White males were under 18 (36 percent compared with 24 percent). One of the circumstances such young people are facing is living in foster care. According to the United States Department of Health and Human Services, of the estimated 542,000 children in foster care nationwide, 37% are African Americans, even though Black youth comprise only 15% of the population 18 years of age and under U.S. (National Clearinghouse 2003).

Another circumstance that the boys in the introductory story represent is that of being detained in juvenile detention centers. It has been estimated that of over 2.5 million juveniles placed in juvenile detention centers, an estimated 60% are either African American or Hispanic (Teplin et al. 2002, 1133). Moreover, a significant number of male youth are being all but abandoned by one or both biological parents and are most commonly being turned over to grandparents or other relatives who are now the primary caretakers. It has already been estimated that at least 12% of Black children nationwide, are being raised by grandparents, and quite often are separated from their biological parents. In some particular communities, the percentages rise as high as 45% (Chase-Lansdale, Brooks-Gunn, and Zamsky 1994, 379).

Homelessness is another difficult reality. The nationwide estimates of homeless youth are between 500,000 and 1.3 million. While Black youth comprise only 16% of all youth in the United States, based on telephone calls it has received from runaway youth, the National Runaway Switchboard estimates that at least 25% of those who are homeless are African American. Of this number, 17% have run away from home. However, for specific localities, the percentages are much higher. For example, based on data of the Florida Network of Youth and Family Services, at least 35% of all youth who have run away from their homes and who have received government services have been Black males, and most are reported as 14 years of age or younger (Richter 2004).

Of course, among the reported dangers of being homeless are physical abuse, sexual abuse, sexually transmitted diseases, and untimely deaths. African American males are now five times more likely to be murdered than White youth. Some surveys of Black homeless youth report their being out of touch with parents, and out of reach of needed emotional and financial support, making them easy targets for recruitment to sell drugs and involvement with criminal behavior. Other surveys report youth describing intense conflicts with one or more people in their families or foster homes, and quite often having been put out of the homes. Others seem to have become homeless within two to four years of exiting either foster care systems or juvenile detention centers.

Many young Black males face the experience of being new to an entire country. Figures from the 2000 U.S. Census indicate that it was during the 1990s that an estimated 41% of the current total population of Black immigrants entered the United States. Another 32% arrived earlier, between 1980–1989, and 27% arrived prior to 1980. The Census reports that 28% of those who entered during the 1990s were Black males from Africa, and 56% were Black males from the Caribbean. While some of the young immigrants have come from formerly British colonies, speaking either English or Patua, others have come from formerly French colonies, speaking French or Creole. This language challenge alone can force a young person into feeling isolated and powerless to make new friends. In some cases, it can even cause the person to become the target of bullies.

In addition to all of the previously mentioned challenges facing young people, Black young people, overall, have been found by many researchers to be lacking in information about their African heritage (Christian and

Barbarin 2001, 43). This is unfortunate, because studies have shown that there is a positive relationship between healthy self-esteem, resilience, upward mobility, and a healthy understanding of and identification with one's African American heritage (Morris 2003, 1). Psychologists such as Naim Akbar, moreover, have noted that the lack of a clear identification of one's relationship to one's heritage can cause and exacerbate emotional and psychological problems (Akbar 1989, 15).

Of course, the total population of young African American males should not be characterized as troubled or at risk. One needs only to read about such annual events as the ACT-SO (Academic Olympics) awards, to identify young Black men who are teenagers demonstrating their gifts as architects, engineers, chemists, inventors, writers, poets, musicians, and cinematographers. What is also good news is that a growing body of national surveys reflects that a statistically significant number of such achievers are receiving spiritual, emotional, and sometimes financial support from churches they attend (Christian and Barbarin 2001, 53).

In fact, as mentioned before, Robert Hill, expert on the Black family, has found that one of the primary factors accounting for resilience and success among African Americans (youth included) is a strong religious orientation (Hill 2003, 135). Moreover, a number of researchers have gathered data that lends support to the notion that it is what they call "religious orientation" of young people that may indeed be a major contributing factor. There is evidence that a large percentage of African American young people live in households where leaders of the home are religious (Boyd-Franklin 2003, 125). Of course, these surveys do not attempt to detect the exact nature of this commitment to the Lord. However, it can be assumed that, in these households, there is, at a minimum, a healthy regard for the existence and power of God.

A number of surveys indicate that a large percentage of African American young people are at the least exposed to such adults who are religious. Again, such surveys do not try to detect or judge the exact nature of the relationship with God. However, the National Survey of Black Americans, conducted by Linda and Robert Taylor, found 93% of Black people saying that they prayed, 82% saying they watched at least one religious program, 74% saying they read religious material of some type, and 83% feeling that Black churches have helped Black people improve their conditions. Sixty-four percent said that they had at some time received some type of support from the church or from church members. Another survey by the Joint Center for Political Economic Studies found that two-thirds of the money that Black people said that they gave to a charity of some type went to a Black church (when churches were classified as charities) (Hill 2003, 119).

In terms of the impact of church involvement on the achievement of young people, Taylor and Chatters found that the more students reported attending church, the more likely they were to be attending school regularly, completing homework, and engaging in positive social activities (Taylor and Chatters 1991, 105). Marcelle Christian and Oscar Barbarin, examining specifically poor Black children and their families from Ohio and southeastern Michigan, found that parents who attended church with their children reported having far fewer conflicts with the children than did parents who did not attend church with their children (Christian and Barbarin 2001, 43).

This study found that the Black church, in general, seemed to be a resource factor that enabled children to become resilient and to bounce back from adversity. The children from church-attending families were found having more confidence in themselves, placing more emphasis on positive extracurricular activities and having higher goals for themselves than students who were not involved in a church. Moreover, they found that children who attended church with their parents were not as likely to exhibit personality traits such as being rebellious (traits that the researchers called "oppositional behavior") as children who did not attend church with their parents. In all fairness, similar results were also found for children who attended other religious institutions than churches (Christian and Barbarin 2001, 43).

These children were also noted as being much less likely to exhibit what the researchers defined as immature behaviors than were children who did not attend church. Taking a closer look at this phenomenon as it related to low income families and communities, Christian and Barbarin studied the connection between "religiosity" and teaching African American young people about their African American heritage. They were interested in the effects of helping young people to both develop a religious faith and to understand the significance of their racial heritage (along with how to deal with racism). They found that the combination of teaching children about their heritage/racial identity and kindling an awareness in children that they personally had internal resources (through their spirituality and gifts) to overcome adversity such as racism, had a positive impact on the children's resilience. However, they discovered that teaching one or the other in isolation did not have as much of an impact and could actually have a negative outcome (Christian and Barbarin 2001, 43).

There have also been a number of studies that have sought whether there was any correlation between Black youth spirituality and the avoidance of a wide range of at risk behaviors such as substance abuse, age at first intercourse, skipping school, and joining gangs. The studies have consistently shown that young people who are involved in church (and other religious institutions) and/or express a faith commitment, are less likely to engage in such at risk behaviors.

Other researchers were interested in whether the influence that the church had on individuals eventually impacted the neighborhoods and communities where the churches were located. Barbarin, for example, found churches to be as community institutions that impact individuals who further impact communities by becoming "resource factors" for surrounding neighborhoods. Such churches were found providing opportunities for entire neighborhoods and communities to experience resilience (i.e., resurrection) from adverse circumstances (Christian and Barbarin 2001, 46). Another study also showed how churches affecting Black youth in communities also reduced crime rates in environments surrounding churches (Johnson et al. 2000, 479).

Wendy Haight was interested in what churches were teaching that had such a positive impact on Black youth. After an in-depth study of interactions between adults and children at First Baptist Church in Salt Lake City, Haight concluded that the church taught a very specific value system, one that equipped young people for successful lives within and outside of the church. First of all, there was the conversion experience and its spiritual significance. When a child made a decision to commit himself or herself to the Lord, the young person acquired the belief that he or she was now in touch, from within, with a divine resource (Haight 2002, 22). That awareness was foundational and very powerful.

The church presented teaching that each person (including children and youth) had gifts that he or she could use in the family, church, school, and community (Haight 2002, 19). They were taught that these gifts are given by the Holy Spirit of God, a lesson that was also very powerful. Then the church also taught an alternative view of reality. It presented how there are divine resources in the "bigger picture" (23). The church also taught young people the connection between the sacred and the secular, that is, how to make practical use of their religious teachings (24). The church provided many examples of spiritual development and resilience through the art of storytelling (29). Above all, the children were able to see their parents, relatives, and parents' friends acting as role models, and serving as ministers, deacons, and officers of the church (28).

Finally, researchers such as Robert Hill, Eric Lincoln, and Lawrence Mamiya studied African American churches to identify specific types of programs that are offered to young people, particularly to young men. After surveying 2,150 Black churches in mainline Black denominations, Lincoln and Mamiya found only 14.7% saying that they had no specific programs for young people. Most churches offered youth choirs, the Baptist Training Unions, evangelistic rallies, and a wide array of educational programs (Lincoln and Mamiya 1990, 309).

Lincoln and Mamiya were also interested in what African American young people encounter in churches. They found that churches expose them to the Black church's traditional self-help tradition. This teaching was being reinforced from the pulpit. Young people from all socioeconomic levels were able to see working adults; this was particularly helpful for poor young people, who lived in areas surrounding so many churches, where there presently may not have been as many working and middle-income African Americans for them to see anymore (Lincoln and Mamiya 1990, 315).

Such young people were helped by observing disciplined adults allocating their personal time to positive activities rather than "hanging out" on street corners, as so many idle youth and adults are often seen doing. Lincoln, Mamiya, and Haight found that Black churches had a positive socializing environment. Lincoln and Mamiya cited a wide range of exemplary self-help church organizations in churches throughout the United States, all of which are examples of the African American church at its best—particularly for working with Black youth (Lincoln and Mamiya 1990, 164).

Of course, for the church to function at this level requires a fleet of obedient adults who are committed to spending their time, talent, and resources to see that such programs are sustained, and will help recruit participants for them.

A CLOSER LOOK AT JESUS AND HIS EARTHLY PARENTS
Luke 2:41–52

Luke 2:41 Every year his parents went to Jerusalem for the Feast of the Passover. **42** When he was twelve years old, they went up to the Feast, according to the custom. **43** After the Feast was over, while his parents were returning home, the boy Jesus stayed behind in Jerusalem, but they were unaware of it. **44** Thinking he was in their company, they traveled on for a day. Then they began looking for him among their relatives and friends. **45** When they did not find him, they went back to Jerusalem to look for him. **46** After three days they found him in the temple courts, sitting among the teachers, listening to them and asking them questions. **47** Everyone who heard him was amazed at his understanding and his answers. **48** When his parents saw him, they were astonished. His mother said to him, "Son, why have you treated us like this? Your father and I have been anxiously searching for you." **49** "Why were you searching for me?" he asked. "Didn't you know I had to be in my Father's house?" **50** But they did not understand what he was saying to them. **51** Then he went down to Nazareth with them and was obedient to them. But his mother treasured all these things in her heart. **52** And Jesus grew in wisdom and stature, and in favor with God and men.

One question that cannot be answered based on this Scripture passage is whether the boy Jesus (similar to the boys in the introductory story) had already benefited from a synagogue-based educational program. That is, did this training occur prior to the time that He actually appeared in this episode of the gospel of Luke? Is it possible that Jesus had already known some of these temple teachers before His parents, Mary and Joseph, found Him talking with them? Had Jesus already been enrolled in something like a Rites of Passage program in one of the synagogues in Galilee before He came with His parents to Jerusalem that day? That is plausible, seeing that it was the custom, among Jews in that day, for children to be taught both at home and at the temple or synagogue. At home, the father would have been responsible for the instruction, and in the temple, the teachers would have assumed the role of instructor (Yarbrough 1993, 43).

As the Son of God, Jesus was omniscient. However, according to custom, by 12 years of age, He would have reached the point of receiving instruction in the Laws of Moses, perhaps in a local synagogue. He would also have been receiving teachings related to the Jewish festivals when His parents came to Jerusalem for the various festivals, including the Passover (Weidemann 1989, 143). This is supported by the presence of stories throughout the Gospels where His parents are seen regularly taking Him to the temple and synagogue (see Luke 2:21–39). It is not shown that He ever revolted against the idea of practicing these traditions on the basis of being the Son of God. Similar to the men in the introductory story, perhaps some of the teachers who were with Jesus in the temple court that day were among those who were committed to conveying the laws, customs, and traditions to Jesus (see Deuteronomy 11:19), and who were proud of what they would have interpreted as both his precociousness and His positive responses to their instruction. But, ultimately, they were amazed at the depth of divine wisdom and knowledge that Jesus demonstrated.

This passage also indicates that, after this incident, Jesus continued to grow in terms of wisdom and in divine and human favor (see Luke 2:52). The "wisdom" that is mentioned might have been alluding to the wisdom teachings that boys received in their homes and in the synagogues—a systematic and organized part of their education, along with their fathers' trades (Yarbrough 1993, 39). In fact, at that time, the synagogue was seen as being in partnership with the parents when it came to educating the children (Peskowitz 1993, 9).

Both Jesus' earthly parents and the teachers in the temple are seen in this passage as having a very high regard for the boy Jesus. Based on studies of Roman literature, inscriptions on buildings, and writings of first century historians, such regard would have stood in stark contrast to the lack of regard for children that seems to have been reflected in Roman culture (Boswell 1988, 58). The abandoning of children was a common practice in Roman culture. Infanticide was also common. Based on economics and/or inconvenience, it was commonplace for a father to decide that a newborn infant would die. The child would then be placed in an open field somewhere to die. This was particularly (but not exclusively) true for infant girls, largely to avoid the bride price that would have to be paid to future husbands (138).

Moreover, it was not uncommon for such abandoned or "exposed" children to be found and taken into slavery, or sold and forced to become prostitutes to support themselves. It was also not uncommon for children to be surrendered to creditors—a practice that was outlawed in the Jewish law (see 2 Kings 4:1–7). The selling of children, of course, was prohibited in the Jewish Law (see Exodus 21:7). This Jewish prohibition was generally still followed in the first century, when Josephus wrote that Jewish law required the raising of all children. However, Boswell notes that the "exposing" of children was practiced by some Jews (in violation of the Mosaic Law) and by some early Christians. It was so common that first century writers were warning men not to go to brothels because they might end up having sexual relations with their own daughters. Apparently incest was considered more immoral than exposing or abandoning the infant in the first place. Of course, practices such as these created a climate of general distancing between parents and children and general disregard for children, unless the child was a chosen heir to an aristocrat or emperor (Boswell 1988, 138).

Roman parents hesitated to bond with children, because they didn't know whether the child would live. Some researchers have estimated that one-third of all children died by 10 years of age. Some have estimated that the average life expectancy for men was 22 years of age and 20 years of age for women. There are estimates that there were 350 infant deaths per 1,000, and only 49% of children saw their 5th birthday. With such statistics, each couple had to bear at least five children in order to increase the chances that two would reach the age where they, in turn, could have children (Wiedemann 1989, 49). This applied to all socioeconomic groups. However, children of the poor were even more likely to die due to malnourishment, particularly following a famine or following a harvest that produced less than the expected volume of crops. In the eyes of His teachers and parents, Jesus would have been seen as rare because He had lived to be 12 years of age. It required a substantial investment of time and nourishment for children to reach the age of 12. The loss of a child of that age was a substantial loss to any family. That could explain some of the anxiety of Mary and Joseph when they thought that Jesus had been lost.

Mary and Joseph's parental attitudes are also in contrast to those in the general Roman culture that surrounded them, in that they seem to have had a more intimate relationship with Jesus. This is contrary to the pattern of

Roman parents distancing themselves, even from children they had decided to keep by turning over their care to nurses. Quite often children were seen primarily in terms of what they could later provide for the parents (that is, taking care of parents in their old age and burying them). A number of scholars agree that some of these latter feelings had also found their way into Greco-Roman Jewish culture of the time (Wiedemann 1989, 176). Regarding peasant farmers (as Jesus' family most likely was), children were also seen in terms of their ability to share the workload on the farms, and in terms of their continuation of the father's craft (in this case, carpentry). They were also seen in terms of their ability to care for their parents in old age—particularly widows who might have been closer to a child's age than to their father's (girls being married at as young as 12 years of age, while boys being married at perhaps 20–25 years of age) (41).

This reality might have been at the forefront of Joseph's mind when he and Mary confronted Jesus about His behavior—prompting Jesus to explain that His real father was God, something that neither Joseph nor Mary would have been able to understand at the time (see Luke 2:49–51).

However, in the mainstream Roman culture, children, women, and slaves were all marginalized, and seen primarily in terms of their uses to the heads of families—the patriarch. These groups were seen as having inferior mental capacities (Wiedemann 1989, 11). In terms of their humanity, they were not generally recognized as equal in worth to adult Roman males. Children were described as deficient, absent of certain adult traits (5). Because their speech patterns were not as well developed as those of adults, they were not seen as fully developed mentally, or capable of making significant contributions to adult understandings. Moreover, because war was a central activity of prime importance, those who could not participate as soldiers were considered inferior and relegated to the margins of the society (17).

Men were seen as the ones who had the "logos" or reasoning abilities. For men, puberty was seen as bringing with it the ability to reason (Wiedemann 1989, 22). However, even then, the reasoning was seen as faulty and was seen as in need of nurturing. It is also for these reasons that women, children, slaves, and old men were put into the social margins of Roman society, and were seen as highly vulnerable. It is also for this reason that emperors often felt obligated to install legislation that would offer various kinds of protection for widows and children. Overall, fathers had the ultimate authority over the members of their households and had the freedom to whip their children, slaves, and women (22).

It is possible that the writer of the gospel of Luke assembled the stories of the young Jesus to make a counter statement to the empire about who was actually the Son of God. Luke's portrait of the child Jesus (both in this passage and elsewhere) consistently places Him at the center of attention, with everyone around Him recognizing, nurturing, and affirming His potential (see Luke 2:5–8, 29–32, 39–40). In this passage, in fact, He is seen as being admired for His ability to reason. The portrait of Jesus here is very similar to those contained in biographies of emperors, where the writer exaggerates the intelligence of the child emperor in order to convince the reader of the emperor's divinity. This was true of biographies that had been written about Augustus Caesar. The writer of Luke, perhaps, decided to include this story from among the ones that he had collected (see Luke 1:1–4) as evidence that Jesus, the peasant preacher (not Augustus), was the one who had actually shown the signs in His childhood that He was extraordinary and indeed the genuine Son of God—not the emperor whose writers had sent out the propaganda that they were the divine ones (Horsley 2003, 53).

What is common in the portraits of the adult Jesus throughout the Gospels, including Luke, is Jesus' positive attitude toward children. As an adult, Jesus' regard for children is shown by His sayings that one must become like a little child to enter the kingdom of heaven (see Luke 18:17, Mark 10:15). His sayings also include warnings against those who despise children (see Matthew 18:10), and warnings against those who "expose" and abandon children (see Matthew 24:15). Throughout the gospel of Luke, children are portrayed in a positive light, being seen filled with the Holy Spirit and destined for prophetic roles (see Luke 1:11–17, 66, 76), being healed, and contributing to Jesus' ministry (see Luke 7:11–17; 9:46–48; 18:15–17; Matthew 14:13–21; John 6:1–13).

BACKGROUND RESEARCH

1. What is a strong argument for church-based educational programs for young people (Deuteronomy 4:9–20)?

2. What evidence is there that Jesus might have benefited from a temple and/or synagogue-based educational program before He visited the Jerusalem temple in Luke 2:41–52 (Luke 2:21, 22, 25–32, 36–39)?

3. Why was it not necessary to abandon children (2 Kings 4:1–7)?
4. Explain the regulations against children (Exodus 21:7–10).
5. What did the teachers admire about Jesus (Luke 2:41–52)?
6. In the book of Luke, how is the image of John the Baptist as a child contrary to common images of children in Roman culture (Luke 1:7, 59, 66, 76)?
7. How are other portrayals of children in the gospel of Luke different from prevailing notions about children in the general Roman culture (Luke 7:11–17; 9:46–48; 18:15–17)?
8. How are the images of children in other Gospels a contradiction of general feelings about children in the Roman culture of the time (Matthew 18:5; 19:13–14; Mark 10:13–14)?

QUESTIONS FOR REVIEW

1. Review the introductory story. In what sense is the support group that these men and boys have formed an extended "family" of "fictive kin"?
2. What words of Jesus can be applied to the "family" that they have created (Matthew 12:46–50)? Explain in detail.
3. Using Scriptures from the questions under "Background Research" for support, provide the rationale for supporting church-based Rites of Passage programs for youth.
4. If you had to argue for a Rites of Passage program that was tailored specifically for a population of young African American males as represented in the introductory story, which statistics from this chapter would you use to support your arguments? Explain in detail.
5. What are some similarities and differences between the environment in which Jesus grew up and that in which African American young people are growing up today?
6. What does adult obedience to God have to do with the potential and survival of African American youth?

RECASTING THE CHARACTERS

Rewrite the introductory story by making it a Rites of Passage program for young women. Create character sketches of several girls that the church could reach through this program. Be sure to have one of the characters in your story explain what adult obedience has to do with the success of such a program.

QUESTION FOR REFLECTION

What can you contribute toward building a sense of "family" among the young people at your church?

BEING RESPONSIBLE VS. BEING IRRESPONSIBLE

The Good Samaritan: Luke 10:30–37

It was the first meeting of the Jefferson Family Reunion Planning Committee. Richard and Angela had called a representative set of family members to gather at Aunt Emma and Uncle Joey's home after church. Most of those present were cousins who had grown close over the years and were accustomed to hanging out together. They were in the same age range—their mid–30s. Many of them had completed college and had very lucrative jobs. Several of them even attended the same church. However, in addition to Aunt Emma and Uncle Joey, Aunt Lucille and Uncle Steve had joined them. Two items were on the agenda: compiling a list of who to invite and determining the location. Each person had brought a list and had made enough copies for everyone present. The first task was for everyone to read the lists and discover any missing names.

"What about Uncle Winston?" Adrienne asked. "I haven't heard from him since I was a little girl. Isn't he Aunt Agnes' grandfather?"

"I don't think anybody knows where he is," Uncle Steve responded. "The last time I heard, he was in a nursing home somewhere."

"What about Daniel?" Malcolm asked. "Shouldn't he be on your list, Carl?"

"No, he is not on my list," Carl said. "His name is off on purpose."

"Why?" Angela asked.

"Because he's locked up," Carl replied. "He's a junkie. Hasn't anybody told you?"

"Something is wrong with that whole family," Uncle Steve said. "I told Janice not to marry Daniel's father, but she went ahead. Most of the kids are probably junkies by now."

"But how did all the kids end up being junkies?" Angela asked.

"They didn't want to follow in their mother's footsteps," Uncle Steve continued, looking over at Aunt Lucille. "Remember how she got that masters degree in education? She married that guy just because he had an education. But they couldn't do anything with those kids."

"Well, you know, maybe we should find a way to communicate with those who are in prison, those in nursing homes, and those with various problems, to let them know that they are still a part of the family, too," Angela remarked.

"Here we go again. Angela, you're always the good–hearted Samaritan," said Carl.

"Well, what about Ann and her family?" asked Stephanie. "Aren't they supposed to be on your list, Carl?"

"Ann, the perpetually unemployed?" Carl asked. "Why put her on the list? Do you want her and her five kids to come and eat up all the food? You know she won't bring anything. She is forever unemployed. She's living off food stamps, Stephanie. What can she contribute? I am not paying for her. Let her stay home."

"But—" Angela started to tell them that she had already invited Ann, when she was cut off.

"If you ask me, we need to leave off all the losers. Most of the ones on my list at least have their names on somebody's church role, and they have jobs. If we are going to ask the pastor to come, we don't want homeless people, crack addicts, prisoners, unwed mothers, people who are shackin' up, and people with mental problems around," Carl said, cutting Angela off.

"Now I see why you've got my middle name," Uncle Steve said and laughed.

"Plus I don't want to find out about any brothers, sisters, or cousins that I didn't know I had—know what I'm sayin'," said Adrienne, laughing. "Let all fornicators and adulterers stay home."

"I agree. This needs to be a holy reunion between those of us who've got some type of religion," said Gwen, who had been quiet.

"That's the trouble," Aunt Emma said, sitting over in the corner. "Y'all got religion and you aint' got no God."

"OK, OK, maybe I have a solution," Angela said. "Maybe we could set up a family trust fund of some type to handle emergencies. This could be something that we could tap into if somebody didn't have the money to come to a reunion, or if somebody dies without insurance—you know, like Uncle Crawford last year."

"You better shut up," Carl said and laughed. "I know you must be joking. Now you want to turn the family into a welfare agency?"

"I disagree with all of you," Malcolm said. "What Bible are you reading? I saw somewhere that to whom much is given, much is expected. It also says that we are supposed to be our brothers' keepers."

"Yeah, and it says judge not, lest you be judged," said Aunt Emma, who had been mostly quiet up until then. "Looks like some of ya'll in here are so heavenly minded that you ain't no earthly good. Y'all need to remember where you come from. Wouldn't none of you have nothin' 'less God gave it to you. Is that the way to show you're thankful?"

Suddenly the room was silent, as everyone looked over to where Aunt Emma was sitting.

A CLOSER LOOK

It is apparent that the extended family in the previous story consists of a variety of individual families with a range of differences in economic means. Nancy Boyd-Franklin, expert on the African American family, has noted that some of this is a result of the dramatic increase, over the past 30 years, in the numbers of individual Black families that are now in the middle-income economic range. The introductory story is consistent with this reality and with national surveys of African American families. The following information is reflected in the March 2002 report on the Black population, published by the U.S. Census Bureau.

In terms of family income, 33% of all Black families reported having incomes of $50,000 or more, with 52% of Black married couples' families having incomes of $50,000 or more. Twenty-seven percent of

Black married-couple families reported incomes of $75,000 and above. However, 58% of Black families headed by women with no spouses present reported incomes of less than $25,000. While African Americans are only 13% of the overall U.S. population, as a group, African Americans comprise about 25% of those living in poverty. Thirty percent of Black children under the age of 16 are living in poverty, compared to sixteen percent for non-Hispanic White children. However, as high as 35% of Black families that are headed by women with no spouse present were found living in poverty (Hill 2003, 25).

In terms of employment, among the 216.8 million members of the U.S. civilian population age 16 and over, in 2002, 12% (25.4 million) were Black and 72% (155.1 million) were non-Hispanic White. Sixty-eight percent of Black men and sixty-two percent of Black women in this age range were employed. However, the overall unemployment rate for Blacks was 11%— twice that of non-Hispanic Whites (5%).

In terms of family structure, among 26.2 million African Americans, 43% reported that they had never married, 10% reported being divorced, and 6% reported being widowed. Only 35% of African Americans reported being currently married when compared to 57% of non-Hispanic Whites. Of 8.8 million Black families, 48% were married-couple families. However, 43% were headed by women with no spouse present, compared to only 9% of families being headed by men with no spouse present. Eleven percent of African American families consisted of five or more members and were headed by a woman without a spouse present. Moreover, reports such as the 2003 *State of Black America*, have indicated that, within the Black population as a whole, throughout the '90s, there has been a steady growth in a distinct Black young adult (ages 30–40) population that have completed college, have lucrative professions, and that may be experiencing a considerable amount of distance from the general Black community.

Experts on the Black family, such as Andrew Billingsley, Robert Hill, Nancy Boyd-Franklin, and Martin and Martin, explain how these differences in the broader Black population manifest themselves in differences among individual families within broader extended Black families. Moreover, Nancy Boyd-Franklin found that most middle-income Black families are the first in their extended families to have entered that income bracket. In fact, she groups such families into four basic types: those who have middle incomes as a result of being the first in their families to acquire professional degrees, those who are three or more generations removed from poverty, those who were born into families that were already in the middle-income range, and those whose grandparents, parents, and current generation are all in the middle-income bracket (Boyd-Franklin 2003, 144).

However, Boyd-Franklin notes that even within these broad categories, there are differences in the ability of given families to maintain their middle-income status. In many cases, their status is very insecure. She notes that, in some cases, it is difficult to pass down the middle–income status to the next generation. This is because being born in a middle-income family may lower the success drive of the next generation. The only way to help such a non–achieving upcoming generation in a family would be to have accumulated wealth that can act as a "cushion"—something that most Black families lack. The failure to maintain accumulated wealth can jeopardize a particular family's overall income bracket, and that of the immediately upcoming generation.

Moreover, researchers such as Robert Hill have pointed out the wide variety of situations external to the African American family that can have adverse impacts on its economic resources—forces that can either prevent families from being able to overcome adverse economic situations or those that can suddenly plunge a working and/or middle-class family into poverty and/or homelessness (Hill 2003, 1).

As indicated in the introductory story, traditionally, economic differences between the individual families within a broader extended family can either work toward unifying the family, or it can cause conflict and nearly irreparable divisions. As seen in the above story, this is certainly the case when spirituality and biblical principles are not being considered as the basis for promoting unity, but are being used to create a negative divisiveness among the families in the extended family network.

There are at least two perspectives. Sometimes those who have achieved middle-income levels are unable to understand how difficult it may be for others to achieve their same middle-level income. In such cases, the middle–income family members' values may have changed to become more like the individualism and competitiveness of the overall American culture. In some cases, their professions may seem to demand it. Martin and Martin make the point that such values may contrast sharply with the values of the traditional Black extended family network, and thereby cause members of their Black family to alienate them (Martin and Martin 1978, 102).

These values would most likely surface in discussions as to whether relatives should be placed in nursing homes, whether given family members should bear the full responsibility of raising their own children and/or paying their bills, and whether "lazy" young adults should be put out of their parents' homes and forced to look for employment. Moreover, the continuous needs of troubled members within the family may be seen by the middle–income person as an attempt to pull him or her down. Nancy Boyd-Franklin then notes that the upwardly mobile members of the family may experience the traditional mutual care system of the Black extended family to become burdensome and draining (Boyd-Franklin 2003, 144). The question for the middle-income family member is how to maintain family connections, how to be a part of the mutual aid system of the extended family, but how not to become overwhelmed by these issues, that is, how to set boundaries.

Some middle-income family members may complain that the person in need does not understand, for example, how often the middle-income person has had to decide between helping a given relative and maintaining his or her own standard of living and/or meeting his or her own basic needs. Some may complain that the person in need may not understand the extent to which given family members had to go into debt in order to maintain their lifestyles and/or pay their basic bills. Some say that the persons in need may not be aware of the fact that the seemingly more prosperous person is essentially living on credit cards and may be no more than three paychecks away from welfare. They say that the family members in need and/or others in the extended family network may be unable to see the precarious positions of many of those in the family who have achieved middle-income levels (Boyd-Franklin 2003, 144).

Matters are often made even more difficult when more prosperous members of families also adopt a theology that says that people are poor essentially because they are lazy and sinful. This understanding is often called the "Prosperity Gospel," which may say that if a person were righteous, that person would prosper financially, would not become ill, and would be able to overcome racism—institutional and otherwise. In other words, more prosperous family members who are also Christians may directly or indirectly project to the less prosperous family member that it is mostly sin that is keeping the person in crisis. In this respect, the more prosperous family member can become like Job's comforters in the book of Job who insisted that the disaster that had come upon Job came because Job had sinned (see Job 4:7). Such more prosperous family members may also ignore all the complex historical and current political and economic realities that make it more difficult for African Americans to achieve, and that are, at the same time, so often outside of the person-in–need's control.

While a "holy hookup" with God can certainly make a difference in a person's life, the Bible does not say that such a relationship will automatically remove the stresses and strains of everyday life that sometimes plunge a person into poverty. Such more prosperous family members sometimes project to others that he or she "pulled him or herself up by his or her own bootstraps" without aid of the Black family or church, and usually this is far from the truth. However, such attitudes can and do cause rifts within Black families.

While Robert Hill and Nancy Boyd-Franklin both concur that usually all income levels within the Black extended family do maintain regular communications with each other, sometimes there are instances where the upwardly mobile person (usually in the first generation to enter the middle-income bracket) separates him/herself from the family and develops an entirely new network of friends and acquaintances, avoiding any reference to his/her lower socioeconomic roots. This may even mean living in a different city, only periodically interacting with the family (Boyd-Franklin 2003, 318).

In contrast to the perspective of the seemingly prosperous member of the Black extended family is that of the family member who is less prosperous and is in need of the mutual aid system of the extended family. Such persons in need may also have a different perspective about what the Bible teaches about Christians helping those who are in need. The person in need may believe that Christianity is best expressed through the mutual care system of the African American extended family network (Boyd-Franklin 2003, 300).

The more traditional elements within the Black family system may also be the ones who are the most likely to be mutually dependent upon the Black extended family network. This may explain the sense of outrage when more successful family members are not a more active part of this system—particularly the younger ones who may have benefited from the emotional and financial support of this system in their quest for an education. In *The Black Extended Family*, Martin and Martin explain that this contrast in perspectives can most often surface when a given family member is in crisis (Boyd-Franklin 2003, 300). The person in need may be surprised and/or outraged at the seemingly selfish responses of some family members who have now acquired a different set of values. Due to the severity of a given need, family members may not be able to accept reasons given for not being willing to respond in the traditional mutual aid style of the extended family network (300).

Martin and Martin and Nancy Boyd-Franklin both point out, however, that there are members within the extended family network who abuse the system, refusing to take responsibility for aspects of their lives over which they could exert more control—particularly when it comes to their reliance on the matriarchs of the families who may be the persons with the least amount of resources (Boyd-Franklin 2003, 288). It is also true that, quite often, the family members who do this are dealing with drug addiction. In such cases, the needier family member may also be the one who is the least likely to reach out to access the most powerful resource that so many African American family members have—a strong personal relationship with God through Jesus Christ.

Martin and Martin found that, in general, family members who have not achieved middle–income status may admire and vicariously identify with those family members who have. However, open affirmation may be withheld unless the seemingly successful family member is willing to share some of their resources with the broader Black family (Martin and Martin 1978, 71).

At the root of the conflict is often a conflict of values—a struggle between the individualism and competitiveness of the broader society, and contrasting views concerning what the Bible says about God on the side of the oppressed. It is also a conflict between the theology of the "survival of the fittest," versus a theology of mutual caring and interdependency—contrasting sentiments for which persons holding each respective view claim they find support in the Bible.

A CLOSER LOOK AT THE GOOD SAMARITAN
Luke 10:30–37

Luke 10:30 In reply Jesus said: "A man was going down from Jerusalem to Jericho, when he fell into the hands of robbers. They stripped him of his clothes, beat him and went away, leaving him half dead. **31** A priest happened to be going down the same road, and when he saw the man, he passed by on the other side. **32** So too, a Levite, when he came to the place and saw him, passed by on the other side. **33** But a Samaritan, as he traveled, came where the man was; and when he saw him, he took pity on him. **34** He went to him and bandaged his wounds, pouring on oil and wine. Then he put the man on his own donkey, took him to an inn and took care of him. **35** The next day he took out two silver coins and gave them to the innkeeper. 'Look after him,' he said, 'and when I return, I will reimburse you for any extra expense you may have.' **36** "Which of these three do you think was a neighbor to the man who fell into the hands of robbers?" **37** The expert in the law replied, "The one who had mercy on him." Jesus told him, "Go and do likewise."

There are many biblical stories that show people in need interacting with people who seem more prosperous, but who may not understand "the bigger picture." The story of the Good Samaritan is an example. The question for this study is whether such a story has insights in it that can be applied to how people within families should relate to one another. In this story, the person who first captivates the reader's attention is the man who is found lying half dead along the road between Jericho and Jerusalem. This man is someone who has suddenly been plunged into the ranks of the "have–not," but, at the time of the assault, possibly he had possessions that the robbers found valuable.

Just as the reader of the introductory story is not given much information about the American society that might have influenced the perspectives of the Jefferson family members, the story in the book of Luke does not provide similar information about the "bigger picture" of the Greco–Roman world setting in which the story of the Good Samaritan is cast.

However, what the priest, the Levite, and the Samaritan needed to recognize was that the economic system of the Roman Empire (i.e., "the world's system") was their common enemy. Further, they may have reacted to the situation differently if they had realized that the principles of the kingdom of God were the ultimate solution to the problem manifested by the robbery, its victim, and the ultimate outcome. Their different reactions to this man's dilemma also suggested that they had different understandings (and applications) of the Scriptures that were available to them at the time.

From the perspective of those who "had not," the robbery itself perhaps reflects a need similar to today. Within the first century context in which the story is set, there would have been people who were prosperous, as well as those who were not. For some, robbery could possibly have been the only means of getting what they needed. The text does not tell whether the person robbed was Jew or Gentile, but the fact that the man was headed for the Jewish temple, down a steep and dangerous decline of 18 miles, hints that he was most likely a Jew.

Robert Horsley, in *Jesus and Empire*, says that the first century was a time of widespread disparities between the rich and the poor, particularly among Romans and Jews (Horsley 2003, 59). In fact, there was an acute grain shortage throughout the Roman Empire of that time (Goodman 1997, 142, 200, 282). Peasants, most of whom lived along the countryside, cultivated such grain. However, their lands had to yield enough grain to provide a surplus beyond the taxes they needed to pay. The surplus is what they lived on. Jews paid taxes both to the temple and to the Roman government (Koester 1995, 76).

If there were to be a famine, or other natural disaster, and the land did not yield the needed surplus, they still had to pay the same level of taxes. Therefore people quite frequently lost their land, were plunged into poverty, and became heavily indebted. Such desperate and unemployed people poured into cities such as Jericho, Jerusalem, and Rome looking for employment, which most would not find. They would not find it because they could not compete with the institution of slavery that was on the rise and was providing free labor (Koester 1995, 57).

Therefore, the empire was filled with desperate, hungry people. The likelihood of being robbed was so high that local militia had to be employed to protect main roads. Even the salaries of the soldiers who guarded the roads were paid for in part by taxing the peasants (Koester 1995, 52). The desperate poor consisted of freed slaves who could not compete with free slave labor, farmers who had lost their land to debt, widows, children, and immigrants from various parts of the empire who were unable to locate a place within the Roman society. Goodman indicates that the early first century was a time of high unemployment in the cities and rising prices. Free unemployed laborers were worse off than slaves, as far as having their basic sustenance needs met (Goodman 1997, 254).

Moreover, Jerusalem, at the time in which the story takes place, would have been perceived by many Jewish peasants as a place where the Jewish aristocrats who were associated with the temple lived. During the early first century, Roman governors directly appointed the temple personnel, particularly the High Priests. Therefore, they might also have been seen in collusion with the Roman government. According to Richard Horsley, some temple personnel even collected taxes for Roman government officials. Over the course of Roman occupation, there had been several revolts concerning violations and disrespect by Roman officials (such as Pontius Pilate) for the temple and its traditions. At various points, this situation had the temple officials and the Roman government at odds with each other (Horsley 2003, 70).

First century historian Josephus, in The Jewish War, points out that both the aristocratic Jewish temple personnel and the peasants were from time to time, and to varying degrees, feeling disrespected by the policies of the Roman Empire. Ultimately they would join forces in the initial stages of the revolt against Rome between 66–70 C.E. (Josephus 1980, 597). However, in the setting in which the story of the Good Samaritan is found, it would have been the lower socioeconomic Jewish peasants whose taxes both supported the temple and were combined with the taxes of peasants throughout the empire to support the Roman government. As a result, the peasants probably felt greatly exploited both by Roman and Jewish aristocrats (Schmidt 1992, 200).

Representatives of these two Jewish socioeconomic classes might not have been able to see that their common enemy was Rome's "new world order" economic policies. They might not yet have been able to see that, in the "bigger picture," there was a spiritual warfare going on and that the victory was ultimately one of a spiritual nature. Consequently, triumph over this adversity had to do with the kingdom of God being manifest on Earth. In other words, people needed to get saved!

According to Richard Horsley, at the time in which the story is set, Rome's "new world order" had also led to political unrest. It was a time of escalating protests among Judeans and Galileans over Roman influence and domination. It was also a time when Rome had to show its military might in order to control the protests. Military might was displayed in lavish festivals (Horsley 2003, 26) and through brutality against protesters. For example, in 4 B.C.E., Roman troops had burned Sepphoris and surrounding villages, enslaving the inhabitants and destroying the village of Emmaus. Massive enslavements of tens of thousands of people around Galilee and the Jordan at the time of Jesus' birth would have left the population who lived in those areas traumatized (29).

However, Rome was not able to stop the revolts, messianic movements, and terrorist groups that had been formed. According to Josephus, nor was Rome able to quiet the unrest that was growing among the temple personnel. The area in Palestine where Jesus was born and ultimately carried out His ministry had been a center of massive enslavement and terror (Josephus 1980, 750). Between 53 B.C.E. and the time that Jesus was born, there had been a series of vast displays of Roman might in the area around Jesus' birthplace and where He carried out His earthly ministry (Horsley 2003, 35). In response to Rome's brutal efforts to put down revolts, Jewish terrorist groups had been forming and targeting power holders, including those in their own Jewish societies. They soon formally organized and called themselves the *Sicarri*, but, at the time of this story, they would have been an unorganized group who were making "hits" such as that of the man lying on the Jericho/Jerusalem road (35). In *The Jewish War*, first century historian Josephus recorded that the Sicarri had been conducting daily murders and assassinations, many of which were carried out in broad daylight (Josephus 1980, 750).

Then there were the perspectives of the Jewish aristocrats—the priest and the Levite who did not have time to be bothered with this man who had been robbed. Both, it appears, were good "church" people. These were people who abided by the law. Like Aunt Emma in the introductory story says, they were so "heavenly minded" that they were no earthly good. In both cases, they saw a half-dead man and walked on the other side of the street so as to avoid violating Jewish purity laws (see Numbers 19:10–13). They seemed blind to the socioeconomic realities that had placed the man on the road and to the implications that this unfortunate circumstance might have for their own safety. Moreover, they seemed blind to the broader realities of their "new world order," a system of oppression thrust upon them by the Romans. No doubt comfortable on the surface, concerning their relationships with their Roman patrons, people in positions such as theirs might have thought, for the moment, that they could put up with a little bit of disrespect—just in order to secure their positions and perhaps get an advancement when the time came.

Perhaps the priest and the Levite comprised the "me generation" of their time, and could see no reason to identify with the poor and needy. Conceivably, similar to the Jefferson family in the introductory story, their best solution to the situation was to distance themselves from the marginal family members who seemed of no benefit to them. Similar to some of the members of the Reunion Planning Committee, they may have been unable to see that any unexpected catastrophic event could plunge all of them into poverty together. Of course, this did happen with the destruction of the temple and Jerusalem (A.D. 66–70).

Obviously the Samaritan man saw the "bigger picture." As in many of the other stories in the gospel of Luke, the person whom one would not expect to act appropriately and in faith is the one who does. The Good Samaritan must have been in touch with the spirit of the Law. Reading "between the lines" of this story, one can imagine this Samaritan somewhere in the crowds that surrounded Jesus when Jesus touched the widow of Nain's son and the young man came back to life (see Luke 7:11–15). Perhaps he either witnessed or heard about Jesus touching Jairus's daughter, bringing her back to life (see Luke 8:41–55). This Samaritan, who also had the five books of Moses, could have realized that Jesus had brought the kingdom of God into the world, and, in God's kingdom, one could now look beyond the restrictions of the Law to take care of the real needs of people.

This Samaritan must have had money. The two Denarii that he gave to the innkeeper was enough to take care of two months' rent in the ancient world! However, the fact that he had money did not prevent him from identifying with the man who was now destitute, having suddenly been plunged into poverty. A person like this Samaritan could have had his "finger on the pulse of the times" and realized that it was time to follow the spirit of the Law (see Luke 10:26–28; 14:2–6). Unlike some of the characters in the introductory story, the Samaritan probably decided to look beyond this man's problem—to both see and respond to his need. The Bible does not say what eventually happened to this man who was rescued by the Samaritan. However, if one were to imagine "Scene II" of this drama, if this man should just happen to be looking for a church, one could imagine him looking for one that demonstrated the Samaritan's compassion.

Perhaps the lesson to be learned from the story of the Good Samaritan is that if we are going to help troubled people in our families (both those with and without money), we are going to have to look beyond people's current conditions (spiritual and otherwise) and both see and respond to their needs. If we would like to win them to Christ, then it is the face of Christ that is exhibited by the Good Samaritan that they are going to have to see in us (both those who have and those who have not).

BACKGROUND RESEARCH

1. What were the purity laws concerning touching dead bodies (Numbers 19:10–13)? Explain how this might have affected the actions of the priest and the Levite.
2. Considering your answer to the previous question, what was Jesus' relationship to the Law of Moses (Luke 7:7–15; 8:41–55)?
3. Can Christians become too "legalistic" in relationships with people? How does this Scripture help to answer this question? Explain (Luke 10:28–31; 14:2–6).
4. What was the medical use of the oil that the Samaritan used in Luke 10:34 (Isaiah 1:6)?
5. Generally speaking, what are some negative feelings that Jews had about Samaritans (Matthew 10:5; John 4:9; 8:48)?
6. The history of interactions between Jews and Samaritans occurred when the Jews returned from the Babylonian Exile. Explain the events that caused division between the two groups (2 Kings 17:24–40; Ezra 4:1–23; John 4:4–9, 20–24).
7. What was one of the most basic disputes between the Jews and the Samaritans (John 4:20)?
8. What are some positive feelings that many Jews had about Samaritans (Luke 17:11–19; Acts 1:8; 8:1–25)?
9. What does the Bible teach about neighborliness (Luke 10:22, 29)?

QUESTIONS FOR REVIEW

1. Review the introductory story. What is the "bigger picture" that some of the characters don't seem to be considering?
2. In what sense is the "bigger picture" mentioned in the previous question a spiritual matter? Explain.
3. Judging from the Jefferson family members' discussion, describe the types of people in their family that are "in"? What types of people are "out"?

4. Based on the conversation in the introductory story, what appears to be two contrasting views of what it means to be a good Christian?
5. Review passages from the Gospels that show Jesus carrying out His ministry in Galilee. Then consider your answer to the previous question. Would Jesus agree?
6. Describe the diversity that now exists within African American families. Is there any hope for maintaining unity within families? If so, what is it? Explain.

RECASTING THE CHARACTERS

Rewrite the introductory story. Give the planners, who are laying the groundwork for this family reunion, different attitudes. How might they be more inclusive of different people in their family? What are some specific ways that they can go beyond some of the family members' difficult situations and both see and respond to their needs?

QUESTION FOR REFLECTION

What can you learn from the material covered in this chapter that applies to your extended family? Explain. What role does God play in all of this?

CREATING FAMILY VS. EXISTING IN A VACUUM

Nathanael and Philip: John 1:45–51

It was the greatly anticipated annual meeting of Rose of Sharon Church. The board of directors, deacons, trustees and heads of all the church ministries were present. At this meeting, the church would begin a discussion about whether to relocate. Brother Rankin, head trustee, had surveyed the addresses of most of the church membership. He had discovered that most did not live in the neighborhood around the church anymore. In fact, closer scrutiny of the list revealed that, over the past 20 years, about 50% of the church membership had changed residences, and there had not been a very large percentage of new members who had remained.

He had also checked attendance patterns. He discovered that while most of those who had changed residences had kept their names on the church rolls, most were also irregular in attendance. About 50% attended mostly on Mother's Day, Easter Sunday, and Christmas. The church records also showed that most of these "commuter" members seemed to have grown up in the church, and many had last names that were the same as those of as many as 10 other members.

After Brother Rankin completed his report, Sister Roundtree gave hers. She had completed a telephone survey of members who were irregular in attendance, and had discovered that most of the commuter members had used at least one of the services of the church over the past five years—services such as wedding coordination, baby baptisms, funerals, and sick visitation. After her report, Trustee Anderson reported that the giving levels had not changed much over the past five years. Members who had changed residences had continued to support the church, and many sent tithes whenever they could not attend.

Sister Samuels, director of Christian education, gave her report next. She had taken a survey of all the youth ministries to get updates on the levels of attendance and participation. She reported that both attendance and participation had declined due to young people not being able to get transportation. She reported that most of the parents of the young people had enrolled them into activities in the neighborhoods where they had moved.

Once Trustee Anderson's report was completed, Deacon Jemison introduced the resolution that began the debate. The resolution was that the church should relocate to an area that was closer to where most of the members now lived.

"It makes sense to me," Sister Samuels said. "We need to move to where the membership is so that we can get greater participation in the youth programs. This year, most of the children who came to Vacation Bible School came from the neighborhood. Our own members didn't support it that much."

"Well, if we move, there won't be any programs for those children," Deacon Reynolds replied. "Has the VBS staff followed up with these kids to get them into some of the other youth ministries? Has anyone contacted their families?"

"Not really," Deacon Wilkinson said. "We see VBS as a way to introduce children to Christ. Whether they eventually go to church is God's and their parent's responsibility. Now if their parents come with them, we always invite the parents back. Otherwise, we don't worry about it. If their parents cared that much, they would come with them. Anyhow, most of the kids I see would not fit in with the children at our church. They are not our type—you know what I mean. We need to focus on taking care of our own."

Then Brother Jenkins suddenly stood up and shouted, "See, that is the type of comment that makes me angry. If you ask me, that is the real reason that the Trustee Board won't give me any more money for my Friday night step team. These kids I work with are from this neighborhood. Looks like we're so busy complaining about letting these kids come on the premises that we forget what this church is all about."

"Hold your temper," Brother Jones, the church security guard, said. "Nobody meant any harm. But those kids you bring around here do look like thugs. Ain't nobody gonna base a decision on whether to move the church on those kids."

"You're right," Brother Robinson said. "This church is not for those kids. We need to take care of our own. Our own kids have enough spiritual problems. There were at least three of our girls that got pregnant last year. These girls come from good families. They are of the type that belong to this church. But we are letting them get away, going after gangsters and junkies."

Brother Jenkins then walked out.

"I don't care if he does walk out," Sister Johnson said. "This isn't a good neighborhood anymore. I can see why people moved. I am getting ready to sell my place and get a condo up north. But I wouldn't want to look for another church at this point in my life. My whole family, since the turn of the century, has attended this church."

"We need new members that are going to take this church back to how it used to be, Deacon Wilkerson said. "We need some youth leaders. You won't find youth leaders in this neighborhood."

"If we don't hurry up and do something, we are going to lose some of our most faithful members," Deacon Reynolds said. "Even the Wednesday night prayer meeting attendance has fallen off."

"Maybe that's the problem," Sister Robinson said, just arriving at the meeting from her job. She removed her sweater and rolled up the sleeves on her uniform. "I just heard the tail end of what you were saying. We need some more prayer up in this place, particularly from the people on these different boards and auxiliaries."

"That's right," Deacon Bridgeforth said, joining in. "Check the record. When this church was first built here, it was in order to meet the needs of the families in this community. One of the main goals was to reach out into the neighborhood and invite people into our church family so that they could know that God loved them, and invite them into God's family."

"Yeah, we need to go back and read the mission of the church again," said Brother Watkins, who had been quiet up until then. "Jesus was not called to save people who are well. He came to take care of those who were sick. The church is supposed to be a hospital. It's supposed to reach out into the community and bring healing to the people, not run away from them."

Just then the pastor walked in to join the discussion.

A CLOSER LOOK

Some of the characters in the previous story are looking around at the challenges posed by the neighborhood surrounding their church. While there are those among them who are excited about joining with Jesus in ministering among the sick and oppressed, there are some who, like the biblical character Nathanael, hesitate to get involved. They are asking questions similar to Nathanael's in John 1:46: Can anything good come out of Nazareth?

However, "Black flight" is not typical of African American churches. Like Philip, in this chapter's Scripture passage, most churches have specialized in signing people up to be disciples of Christ. Discussions, such as the one's in the story, do occur, though, when church leadership finds itself unable to identify with the purposes of Christ's church. Such discussions are easiest to occur in situations where most of the members of the church are "commuter" members who have moved to higher income areas of the city or suburbs, with income levels that exceed those of most people in the communities surrounding their churches.

National studies have shown that rather than fleeing low–income communities, Black churches have been developing significant social programs that have been impacting Black communities all over the country. They have not abandoned what most consider their primary calling (that is, facilitating an unbeliever's connection with God through salvation and spiritual development). However, the pastors and members of churches are responding to God's call to minister to the "whole person" and the "whole family." These social action programs have caught the attention of scholars on the Black church such as Andrew Billingsley, R. Drew Smith, Anthony Pinn, C. Eric Lincoln, and Lawrence Mamiya.

R. Drew Smith, in *Long March Ahead*, and Andrew Billingsley, in *Mighty Like a River*, both begin by highlighting the history of the Black church's involvement in outreach to people and families in its immediately surrounding communities. This pattern dates all of the way back to slavery. During slavery, for example, the Black church (sometimes referred to as the "invisible institution") met outside of the reach of the plantation owners, in the middle of the night, to worship God. It is in this environment that plots to help people escape from slavery were developed. It is also the environment where slave revolts were planned. Smith also highlights the involvement of free African Americans and their churches in the abolitionist movement. The aforementioned scholars draw attention to the Black church's involvement in the Civil Rights Movement that spanned the first three quarters of the twentieth century (Smith 2004, 1; Billingsley 1999, xxiii).

In terms of reaching out to the communities surrounding individual Black churches today, Billingsley found that most Black churches have some type of outreach into their communities. He found the number of outreach programs varying by size of church and/or resource level. He also determined that the churches with more resources were able to have more outreach programs that were sponsored (Billingsley 1999, 145).

Anthony Pinn, in *The Black Church in the Post-Civil Rights Era*, found Black churches paralleling Jesus' healing ministry to individuals and families by attempting to address the general health care needs of both church members and people from the surrounding community. These efforts included health care professionals distributing information about health care, making referrals, and administering and teaching about various methods of prevention. Churches also announced available health care resources in bulletins, sponsored physical exercise nights, and supported sports teams in an effort to keep children active by promoting good health through physical exercise (Pinn 2002, 101).

On a larger health care scale, one "mega church" actually constructed an alternative hospital to deal with the crisis of overcrowded emergency rooms in its community. By 2002, in cooperation with a local university, the hospital had seven doctors, two nurses, and four medical assistants. This particular hospital also emphasizes the relationship between a healthy spirit and a healthy body. A pastor of another mega church in New York has organized a collection of 50 churches that have developed affordable housing for its communities, has built health care facilities, and offers medical treatment for the uninsured (Pinn 2002, 73).

Paralleling Jesus' ministry of driving out "demons," Black churches throughout the country have been impacting individuals and families by offering a variety of anti-drug programs. One church out of Los Angeles has an annual meeting of over 2,000 at risk children. At this conference, the church leaders disseminate information and offer resources and referrals that deal with various at risk aspects of the children's lives. On a larger scale, a mega church in New York has a "Safe Space" concept that offers employment, and mentors as many as 500 young people, most of whom are from the community. The program has seen numerous lives change from criminal activity and drug dealing to a more God-centered and God-conscious existence. Another church out of San Diego, California, encourages recovering drug addicts to spend time in conversation with drug dealers and abusers, sharing their personal experiences of salvation and encouraging others to make similar commitments. Yet another mega church out of Detroit is cooperating with the Local Council of Baptist Pastors in building an employment training program in auto mechanics to provide employable skills (Pinn 2002, 95).

Anthony Pinn also found Black churches organizing to protest local city, state, and national issues that adversely impact the lives of Black people and Americans, in general. Their concept of community has expanded beyond the individual church neighborhood. One form that this movement has taken is the fight against environmental racism. Churches involved explained that they see this as an extension of Jesus' healing ministry. For example, Pinn quotes Rev. Dr. Garth Baker-Fletcher as encouraging churches to recognize the relationship between racism and the destruction of the neighborhoods of people of color. He quotes Rev. Dr. Emilie Townes as calling attention to the fact that 60% of the Black population lives in communities where one or more uncontrolled toxic waste dump sites are located. She calls attention to the fact that at least 15 million African Americans live close to more than one such dump site (Pinn 2002, 83; Goldman 1987, 7). Statistics show that the resulting environmentally related health risks are not randomly distributed throughout the population. Communities of color have been shown to bear a disproportionate percentage. As a result, many pastors see protesting this situation as participating in Jesus' healing ministry to families (83).

While various Black churches and denominations have been slow to address this particular health care issue, Pinn has documented individual and collective efforts of Black churches in cooperation with national organizations such as the National Council of Churches and the United Church of Christ Commission for Racial Justice to protest at the local, state, and national levels. Individuals and their churches have put related information in denominational magazines, church bulletins, church newsletters, and have approached local newspapers about carrying investigative reports. Social justice ministries in local churches have also collectively voiced their concerns about environmental hazards (Pinn 2002, 84).

Long March Ahead is a two-volume work by R. Drew Smith that investigates the degree to which African American churches are involved in shaping public policy as it impacts the Black community, communities of color in general, and America at large. He and 30 other scholars researched Black churches over a period of three years. The group surveyed 1,956 churches in 19 major cities, and 26 small rural Southern counties. Ninety percent of the respondents were pastors. The survey tried to detect the extent to which churches were willing to move beyond using their voting capacity to collectively lobby against city, state, and national governmental organizations concerning policy issues that impact individuals and Black families (Smith 2004, 9).

One of the findings identified the difficulty that most Black churches experience when they attempt to stretch their resources to cover lobbying activities. This was found to be largely due to the highly sophisticated and technologically demanding nature of twenty-first century lobbying. However, Black churches throughout the country were found lending various levels of support to lobbying groups concerning issues of significance to the well-being of their individual Black communities and to the national Black community (Smith 2004, 10).

Intercessory prayer is still a large part of the ministries of local Black churches, who overwhelmingly believe that God is a healer. However, the concept of healing has expanded beyond applications to individuals and specific families, to applications to collections of families in communities. Black churches recognize the connection between healthy spirits and healthy bodies. The top priority is directly related to faith activation. They want to say, along with the Lord Jesus, "Your faith has made you whole," regardless of whether a particular disease, such as cancer, dissipates. Moreover, pastors and churches throughout the country have become health care advocates on a number of levels, depending on the resource level of the particular church. Such pastors see this type of activity as a way of partnering with Jesus in facilitating the spiritual and physical healing of individuals, families, and entire communities.

A CLOSER LOOK AT NATHANAEL AND PHILIP
John 1:45–51

John 1:45 Philip found Nathanael and told him, "We have found the one Moses wrote about in the Law, and about whom the prophets also wrote—Jesus of Nazareth, the son of Joseph." **46** "Nazareth! Can anything good come from there?" Nathanael asked. "Come and see," said Philip. **47** When Jesus saw Nathanael approaching, he said of him, "Here is a true Israelite, in whom there is nothing false." **48** "How do you know me?" Nathanael asked. Jesus answered, "I saw you while you were still under the fig tree before Philip called you." **49** Then Nathanael declared, "Rabbi, you are the Son of God; you are the King of Israel." **50** Jesus said, "You believe because I told you I saw you under the fig tree. You shall see greater things than that." **51** He then added, "I tell you the truth, you shall see heaven open, and the angels of God ascending and descending on the Son of Man."

Nathanael asked the question: "Can anything good come out of Nazareth?" Archaeologists vary in their estimates of the number of people who might have been living in Nazareth when Jesus was growing up. The estimates are anywhere from 200–500 people (Ferguson 1993, 386). Most agree, though, that compared to the huge cities built by Herod Antipas in Galilee, Nazareth was seemingly insignificant. It was never mentioned in the Hebrew Bible (Old Testament). First century historian Josephus never mentions it and it was not counted among the plots of land given out by Joshua in Joshua 19:10–15. Even though early Jewish rabbis mentioned 63 other Galilean towns, Nazareth was never mentioned. In fact, its name begins to appear in early Christian literature outside of the New Testament only after the fourth century, when Christianity became the official religion of Rome (Strange 1992, 1050). This, of course, reflects the upper-class biases of the writers who composed earlier literature. That is why Nathanael's class bias concerning Nazareth was not unique. Nazareth had been marginalized.

Nazareth would not have been a favorite location for any young man who was exploring whether there was any possible way to become upwardly mobile. Virtually no reconstruction had been done in the town of Nazareth. Richard Horsley, in *Jesus and Empire*, notes how families prior to the Greco-Roman era had been able to grow a variety of crops, and to subsist based on them. However, Rome had forced them to replace such subsistence farming with a few basic cash crops. These were the crops that were mostly paid out in taxes. This had forced the farming families to use the surplus that they grew to trade even for food. If a famine or some other unforeseeable disaster had reduced the amount of crops they could grow, such families would be plunged into poverty. Such families were also in danger of losing their lands in this manner (Horsley 2003, 111).

Most Jewish families in these small villages like Nazareth were paying the majority of what they grew to a combination of the Roman Empire, King Herod, and the temple in Jerusalem. Crossan notes the evidence that these extended families still kept the Jewish religious traditions. No archaeological digging so far has unearthed an elaborate synagogue building in Nazareth dating back to the first century. The synagogue that is referenced in the Gospels would have been a village gathering or assembly (see Luke 4:16–30). Unlike buildings unearthed in the more affluent Sepphoris, the houses in Nazareth seem to have all disappeared, leaving the impression that they were made of much less expensive materials than those in the wealthier cities and communities. Although there was enough space between houses for livestock, archaeologists estimate that the residents of Nazareth ate mostly grain, oil, and grapes. Essentially, they were poor (Zukeran).

Horsley also notes that the villages in the area where Jesus grew up were places that terrorist were suspected as living. It was an area where a variety of messianic and terrorist movements were developing, movements that would, along with movements outside of Galilee, soon culminate in an all-out revolt against Rome (66–70 C.E.). This revolt would result in yet another destruction of the Jerusalem temple and the scattering of Jews throughout the Jewish Diaspora (Horsley 2003, 39).

By any stretch of the imagination, Nazareth was not what any self-respecting Jewish aristocrat would call a "good neighborhood." Neither was Capernaum, where Jesus chose to carry out so much of His ministry. Jonathan L. Reed, in *The Population of Capernaum*, notes that Capernaum was not a popularly sought out spot. But it did have a somewhat more developed village. In fact, archaeologists have discovered that its inhabitants might have relied on both agriculture and fishing, but they also had to pay most of the proceeds from both occupations to Rome, to Herod, and to the temple aristocracy (Freyne 1980, 38). In fact, based on the stories in the Gospels, Capernaum also appeared to have been filled with sick and hungry people (see Matthew 8:5; Mark 1:21; Luke 4:16–24; John 4:46–53).

Apparently Jesus decided to reach out and minister within His communities and the troubled communities close by. Based on the Gospel stories, Jesus appears to have spent most of His childhood with His earthly family in Galilee, in Nazareth. It also appears that He spent some of His adulthood ministering in Nazareth, but most of it in places like Capernaum, and other small nearby villages (Strange 1992, 1005). Like the board members in the introductory story, Jesus at some point probably had to decide whether He would minister in this location on seek some wealthier town. One might be tempted to speculate why the Son of God would not have chosen to spend most of His time ministering in the "higher octave" (from a material point of view) of Sepphoris or Tiberias. However, anyone who knows Jesus, the Son of God, knows that He was on a divine mission. We know it was because God so loved the world, that he gave his only begotten son, that whosoever believeth in him should not perish, but have evelasting life (John 3:16, KJV). Jesus, in fact, had come to reach those who would receive Him—rich and poor alike.

Nazareth and Capernaum were only two of many nearby communities. Probably the most exciting among the other choices to any given young man from Nazareth could easily have been Sepphoris and Tiberias, the two successive Roman capitals of Galilee (Crossan 2001, 4, 33). Sepphoris was only a distance of four miles (about one hour's walking distance) from Nazareth (much closer than Capernaum). According to John Dominic Crossan and Jonathan L. Reed, in *Excavating Jesus: Beneath the Stones, Behind the Texts*, Herod Antipas had rebuilt Sepphoris in 4 B.C.E. The city had once been burned to the ground by Roman soldiers in response to a rally that the Jewish inhabitants held against foreign rule and taxation that had been conducted around 4 B.C.E. The city that Antipas had rebuilt was nowhere near as elaborate as various cities such as Caesarea Maritima built by Herod the Great. However, Nazareth, the village where Jesus had grown up, was no comparison to either of these cities (4, 17, 33).

It is difficult to speculate how poor young men from villages such as Nazareth might have perceived a glamorous city like Sepphoris. At the time it was a city of rich Jewish aristocrats and some Gentiles. If Jesus had not been the Son of God, with a divine mission, as a youngster coming out of Nazareth, Sepphoris might have seemed like a much more glamorous site to fashion some sort of "ministry." Had Jesus not thought the way in which He did because of His divine purpose, maybe He would have compromised and given up on the notion of being a Messiah, and/or "dying for people's sins." If it could be had by a poor Jewish farmer, perhaps there might have been a slim chance for a lifestyle in Sepphoris that would have been much more attractive, and that would only have required walking through the magnificent city square and merely "pontificating." In this scenario, all that would have been necessary was to "pay one's dues," get an aristocratic Roman or Jewish patron, and soar ahead as a philosopher. Galilee, particularly Sepphoris, was known as a location of philosophers called cynics (Crossan 1994, 114). A young man could easily be attracted to this occupation; however, there is no evidence that cynics were being crucified in any large number.

To the people of Nazareth, the city of Sepphoris might have been just as appealing as some middle-class areas were to the board members in the introductory story. Archaelogists have discovered that this city had an elaborate Roman-style theater, with Roman columns and a central city square similar to a forum. Its streets and buildings were covered in marble, and its buildings had mosaic floors. While mostly aristocratic Jews lived there, Herod Antipas had imposed Greco-Roman architectural style on the area, accented with plenty of mixed Jewish and pagan symbolism. Further, Sepphoris had become Galilee's largest city, and, along with the city of Tiberias (which Antipas also built), it stood out with the Greco–Roman architecture in Jewish Galilee. Moreover, Sepphoris was walled in with visible white walls (Reed 2002, 5).

Capernaum seems to have been much larger than Nazareth, with a population estimated at around 1,000, compared to 8–12,000 for cities like Sepphoris and Tiberias. Jonathan Reed, in *Kingdom Building in Galilee*, noted that archaeologists have found the architecture in Capernaum of the first century to have been about as simple as that in Nazareth (Reed 2002, 10). While Capernaum seems to have had a more architecturally developed location for its synagogue, it had no theaters, no hydrodomes, no administrative complexes, no temples, and it was mostly not populated by aristocrats (Crossan 2001, 81). The discovery of a house and a boat, dating back to the first century CE (which some have interpreted as belonging to the apostle Peter), has provided indications of the relatively desperate lives of people living in Capernaum—lives that could in no way be compared to the lavish lifestyles of aristocrats in Sepphoris and Tiberias (Reed 2002, 10).

Yet, Jesus elected to call His disciples, and to minister and teach among the poor, sick, and oppressed, primarily in Nazareth, Capernaum, and other small villages. Apparently Nathanael and Philip decided to allow Jesus to change their lives, become His disciples, and join in with the type of ministry that He was doing among the poor.

Church leaders today such as those in the introductory story would do well to follow Jesus' lead and make the decision to continue reaching out to the needy communities in which they find themselves. In the end, they will gladly hear Jesus, the model Servant, address them by saying, "Well done, my good and faithful servants."

BACKGROUND RESEARCH

1. What aspect of Jesus' Capernaum ministry is portrayed in the gospel of Mark (Mark 1:21–28; 2:1, 11, 14; 9:33)?
2. What is the relationship between Jesus and Capernaum portrayed in the gospel of Matthew (Matthew 4:12–22; 8:5–13; 9:1)?
3. What can we learn from the image of Jesus' ministry in Capernaum that is presented in the gospel of Luke (Luke 4:23, 31–39; 7:1–10)?
4. What can we learn from the image of Jesus' ministry in Capernaum that is presented in the gospel of John (John 4:46–54; 6:26, 59; 7:1; 10:15)?
5. Usually Jesus' teachings had more than one layer of meaning. In the Lord's Prayer, are there any allusions to socioeconomic conditions (Matthew 6:9–13; Luke 11:2–4)?
6. What insights about the poor are revealed in Jesus' teaching in Matthew 7:7–11 and Luke 11:9–13?
7. In addition to other meanings, what insights about labor conditions in the countryside might be revealed in Matthew 20:1–15 and Luke 16:1–8?
8. Read Leviticus 25, with particular attention to 25:23. Then read Luke 4:16–17. In what subtle ways might "the year of the Lord's favor" relate to the Leviticus passage? In what ways might the aristocratic landowners

who seized people's lands and sold them to earn money be a violation of a sacred tradition among Jewish people? Explain.

9. In what types of settings did Jesus' healings typically take place (Mark 5:21–43)?

QUESTIONS FOR REVIEW

1. What are the two opposing viewpoints that are represented in the story at the introduction to this chapter? In what ways are they similar and/or different from the views of Nathanael and Philip when Philip first extended an invitation to Nathanael?
2. What is the central issue?
3. What are the strengths and weaknesses of each side of the argument?
4. What has been the characteristic response of African American churches to community outreach? Is there room for improvement? If so, in what ways?
5. What does it mean to respond to the "whole person" or the "whole family"?
6. Does the church have to choose between reaching a person/family for Christ and addressing a person/family's socioeconomic and political needs? Is it a matter of either/or or both/and?
7. In what ways are the organizations in local African American churches that you know about consistent with or in contradiction to Jesus and the disciples' earthly ministry in Galilee?
8. Does Jesus still have an earthly ministry? Explain.
9. In what sense is the church a large extended family? Explain.

RECASTING THE CHARACTERS

Pretend that you are the pastor who has walked in to join the discussion in the introductory story. What would you say? Would the contents of this chapter help you? If so, how?

QUESTION FOR REFLECTION

What can you learn from the material covered in this chapter that applies to your church family? What role does God play in all of this?

THE FAMILY REUNION: WITH GOD VS. WITHOUT GOD

The New Heaven and New Earth: Revelation 21:1–7

Finally the day had arrived. The Jefferson Family Reunion Committee had been planning for months. This was going to be SOME Jefferson family reunion. It had taken quite a bit of work to bring all of the different segments of this family back together again. There was no promise that the family would get through the weekend without a fight, but the committee was hopeful that the forces of unity would prevail over those of disunity. While there were members of the family that had not been speaking, the planning committee was hoping that tonight would be the beginning of something new.

The weekend was to begin with a church service and a talent show. This "Jefferson Family Hour" had been announced in the past Sunday's bulletin. Each month the church celebrated a different family. The pastor had said that he expected most of the church members to come to the service, because the Jefferson family was one of the founding families of the Rose of Sharon church, dating all the way back to the turn of the twentieth century. By now, almost everyone knew people from this family.

The plan was that the reunion would begin with a church service that included a talent show, and a presentation of the family's story. This would be followed by a potluck in the church cafeteria. On Saturday morning, the Jeffersons would have a picnic. Then, on Saturday night, they would take a boat cruise. On Sunday morning they would come back to church again, and would end the reunion with a Sunday afternoon brunch.

All the members of the Jefferson Family Reunion Planning Committee were there wearing red vests. As 7:00 p.m. arrived, the Jefferson family slowly began filling the chapel. As people walked in, they could see the planning committee members moving around, greeting people and making sure everything was in place. Angela had just placed the last ribbon on the end of one of the pews where the family members were to sit. Brother Jenkins was waiting out in the lobby with the step team. He was beaming because this was the first time that they would perform, since the Trustee Board had funded their uniforms. Some children from the neighborhood who had recently joined the church were on the team, and several of the young people from the Jefferson family were also on the team.

As master and mistress of ceremonies, Carl and Angela had just taken their seats on the pulpit beside the pastor when the women's chorus came down the aisle and entered the choir loft. The pastor began the service with prayer and then turned the program over to Carl, who greeted those family members who had arrived and set out the agenda for the weekend. He then turned the program over to Angela, who would host the family story segment of the program. Carl was just taking his seat when the back door of the church opened, and in walked Ann with her five children. Carl hadn't seen her for years. Ann and her children took their seats with the other Jeffersons.

After a song from the women's chorus, Dennis, the family historian, presented a fantastic video presentation. It told the family story with pictures, maps, and music. There was seemingly no end to the "oohs" and "aahs" and the clapping. Then Angela announced, "It's testimony time, folks! During the next thirty minutes, we would like anyone who wishes to share a personal story about something that God has done in your life. We all know that we can never praise God enough for the things God has done."

Several people walked up to the microphone and gave their testimonies. Then Ann remembered that just this last Sunday, she had promised God that she would never hesitate to tell her story. She had promised never to be ashamed of what God had done for her. So she walked down the aisle, stood behind the microphone, and faced the congregation.

She then motioned with her hands for her children to come forward. "I would like to begin my testimony with a song," she said. The children, who had formed a small quintet, sang, "Hallelujah, Jesus

Saves!"—a song Ann had learned from her Aunt Emma when she was a little girl, and in turn had taught it to her children.

Ann then told the story of how she had been like the woman at the well, looking for love in all the wrong places, until she had found Christ. Surrounded by her children, she told of how she had a little talk with Jesus and how Jesus had made everything all right. She told of how she and each of her children had accepted Christ as their personal Savior. The children then sang one final verse of the song and walked toward their seats. Just then, the church musician spontaneously began playing some music on the organ, and Ann looked over just in time to see Aunt Emma doing the holy dance. As Ann sat down, she caught a glimpse of Carl, her older brother, wiping tears from his eyes with a white handkerchief. The women's chorus then spontaneously broke out in song, as the Holy Spirit of God took over the worship service. Ann would never ever forget this night.

A CLOSER LOOK

The introductory story is the last of several episodes from the Jefferson family. In the first, Ann had accepted Jesus Christ as her personal Savior. In another, the Jefferson Family Reunion Committee was trying to plan a reunion that would eliminate anyone who had any problems that would embarrass them in front of their church. In yet another episode, the board members of the church, where the Jefferson family had been attending for years, were discussing whether it should relocate. In the current episode, something seems to have happened. Everyone in the family appears to feel welcome. The church itself seems to have taken on a new attitude. Even though there may still be splits in the family and rifts in the church, it seems like the family and the church are headed toward a unity that is empowered by the Holy Spirit of God.

A very powerful vision seems to be driving this family, even though different ones might only have small pieces of it. Angela, for example, might have a desire that everyone in the family will feel a part of it. Dennis might have a passion that the family members will know the story of how they got over and that in itself might give the family something for which to thank God. Ann might now have a desire for people to be "real" and refrain from gossiping about one another, but will make themselves available when someone needs help. Aunt Emma might have a yearning that people will remember where they came from, and that they will know the difference between having religion and having God. Finally, Carl might have the longing for people to hold themselves to certain standards of behavior, and that they will know that in God, all things are possible. When all of the pieces are put together, this is a very powerful picture, and it is no wonder that, already, the family is on its feet praising God.

This is also remarkable, when one considers the pressures that are operating against African American families and churches. These are indeed burdens that in some ways resemble the forces of evil that are captured in the book of Revelation. The introductory story provides one "close–up" look at one family, worshiping within one church. However, if the camera lens were to "zoom out," there would be a broader context. Consider the many pressures that are reflected in the following summary of data taken from the 2000 United States Census Bureau American FactFinder report and from other sources. It is possible to locate similar data for many Black churches scattered throughout various urban landscapes.

While it is understood that the summary of these reports are certainly alarming and depressing, it is useful to soberly consider them here, in order to get a realistic picture. They force us to make choices—are we going to lend our time, talents, and treasures to perpetuate the building of a world's system that pits us against each other in competition and ignores the poor and needy? Or are we going to lend our resources to building God's kingdom where people can be saved, healed, and can, in turn, add their talents to God's kingdom–building project? Of course, for families like the Jeffersons and for churches like the Rose of Sharon, it is not going to be easy.

Of the residents of this particular zip code, 97% are African Americans, compared to 12.3% nationwide. The median value of the homes, as well as the residents who own their homes, is well below the national level. There is a shortage of males compared to females, with low percentages of both males and females in residence who are married when compared across the nation. Thirty-one percent have disabilities, compared to nineteen percent nationwide. Each person in this area earns an average of $13,916 compared to $21,587 nationwide. Moreover, 31% of the residents live below the poverty level, compared to 12.4% nationwide (U.S. Census Bureau). If we were to "read between the lines," we could see people suffering, and we would become aware of a very unequal distribution of resources, in a very rich country.

At this point, let us pause for a moment to reflect on this data and prayerfully ask God to show us by, the Holy Spirit of God, how we as a people—individuals and congregations alike—can begin to work together to counteract this situation. By doing so, we, as the church, can begin to make a difference with the help of God, who has all power, strength, and wisdom.

"Zooming out" farther, a profile of the crime statistics reveals quite a bit of criminal activity—another pressure on Black families and churches. For example, in 2004, there was a wide disparity between crimes committed in this area compared to the nationwide figures (AreaConnect). Again, reading between the lines reveals some very desperate people, perhaps, in part reacting to the unequal distribution of resources.

One cannot ignore the pressures that bear down upon a family whose loved ones are in prison. It is noteworthy that most of the imprisoned are descendants of people who were brought to America as slaves, held in bondage, and after emancipation, still had to face discrimination, segregation, and the persistent unequal distribution of resources. Can we not find the answer that will redirect Black people away from a life of crime and toward the pursuit of education? God has already spoken and identified an important key to restoration and wholeness when God said, "My people are destroyed from lack of knowledge" (Hosea 4:6).

Zooming out to the national level, there is the rampant problem concerning the AIDS pandemic. Even though African Americans comprise only 13% of the United States population, in the year 2000, African Americans accounted for half of all newly reported AIDS cases (Fitzpatrick 2004, 14). This statistic applies to people of African descent in the Americas. However, if the camera were to "zoom out" to take in the international landscape, the state of people of African descent throughout the world is also alarming. The statistics on the AIDS pandemic alone are staggering. Worldwide, in the year 2000, 5 million people were infected with the HIV virus at the rate of 15,000 per day. That is 11 infections per minute! Globally, by the year 2000, 35 million people worldwide were living with AIDS. However, of that number, 25 million live in Sub–Saharan Africa! In its wake, AIDS is one of the primary factors contributing to a decline in life expectancy across Africa.

The Joint United Nations Programme on HIV/AIDS has projected that between 2005 and 2010, the life expectancy in Sub–Saharan Africa will decline from 59 to around 44 years (Poku and Cheru 2001, 37).

When deaths due to AIDS are added to deaths due to other diseases, to the lack of available medicines, and to deaths in civil wars, a very disturbing picture emerges. It is a picture of how a worldwide system of unequal distribution of critical resources between poorer and wealthier nations can trigger violence and destruction among the victim's themselves. People of God, we cannot allow ourselves to ignore this situation and behave as though this is someone else's problem and there is nothing for us to do. At the very least, we can invoke God's help and call on the name of Jesus to show us exactly what we can do to alleviate so much suffering and pain. Let us keep our focus on the One who can make all the difference: "For nothing is impossible with God" (Luke 1:37).

The previous gruesome statistics have been presented in order to create a sense of reality. Directly and indirectly, these pressures cannot help but be felt by people such as the Jefferson family and the members of Rose of Sharon church, mentioned in the introductory story. In any given family, seemingly impersonal forces, such as those represented by the statistics, can become personal in the form of substance abuse, jealousy, near hatred, violence, child abuse, pregnancies at early ages, and acquiring sexually transmitted diseases.

On a positive note, in the Jefferson family, one can see the beginnings of a unity and a developing vision that will equip them to fight against outside forces that have the potential to tear the family and church apart. People are committing their lives to Jesus Christ. From their commitment to God and the Word of God, they are getting a vision. The vision that is unfolding involves unity and commitment to each other and to their church. Through forgiveness, prayer, and care for one another, they are renewing the ties that can bind their family together. Moreover, from a position of strength, perhaps the families of this church ultimately will be able to reach out into the world and become agents of God in global transformation—reaching all the way to Africa. Not even the sky is the limit for what we can do if we commit our money, talent, and time to God's wisdom and care. What this family and this church are beginning to piece together is the kingdom of God, on Earth, among them! After all, the people of God will prevail and triumph, as victory awaits at the end of God's plan for humanity (see Revelation 21)!

God also gave the author of the book of Revelation a powerful vision of what God can do, even though he also was surrounded by a troubled world system.

A CLOSER LOOK AT THE NEW HEAVEN AND THE NEW EARTH
Revelation 21:1–7

Revelation 21:1 Then I saw a new heaven and a new earth, for the first heaven and the first earth had passed away, and there was no longer any sea. **2** I saw the Holy City, the new Jerusalem, coming down out of heaven from God, prepared as a bride beautifully dressed for her husband. **3** And I heard a loud voice from the throne saying, "Now the dwelling of God is with men, and he will live with them. They will be his people, and God himself will be with them and be their God. **4** He will wipe every tear from their eyes. There will be no more death or mourning or crying or pain, for the old order of things has passed away." **5** He who was seated on the throne said, "I am making everything new!" Then he said, "Write this down, for these words are trustworthy and true." **6** He said to me: "It is done. I am the Alpha and the Omega, the Beginning and the End. To him who is thirsty I will give to drink without cost from the spring of the water of life. **7** He who overcomes will inherit all this, and I will be his God and he will be my son.

John's vision of a new Heaven and a new Earth can best be appreciated if considered against a backdrop of the times in which John is believed to have composed the book of Revelation. For Jews, Gentile Jewish converts, Christian Jews, and Christian Gentiles, it must have seemed as if the world was coming apart all around them. Any statistics from those days would have been at least as depressing as those quoted in the preceding paragraphs.

The book of Revelation itself is believed to have been composed during two periods—the first around the time of the Jewish War with Rome of 66–70 C.E. when Jerusalem fell and the Jewish temple was destroyed. The second was during the final decade of the first century (Ehrman 2003, 460). That is, it would have been written as the Jews were gradually heading toward another war with Rome, to take place between 132 and 135 C.E. These two periods were also periods of intense persecution of Christians at the hands of Emperors Nero (54–68 C.E.) and Domitian (81–96 C.E.). It was under Nero that Paul, Peter, and James, the brother of Jesus, are believed to have been martyred (Crossan 2004, 40).

Moreover, it was during the reigns of Nero and Domitian that the famous Roman gladiators reached a peak of their popularity. Nero spent huge amounts of money that built the theaters where the gladiatorial contests took place. It was in those contests that Christians, slaves, Jews, and women were pitted against and eaten by lions and other animals. This was a favorite pastime of many Romans. It was also during Nero's reign that Rome became a center of festivals and circuses for homeless and impoverished peasants (Koester 1995, 380).

The book of Revelation opens with letters to seven churches in Asia Minor (Ehrman 2003, 461). Similar to the Jefferson family, the extended families in these churches were surrounded by the chaos of the world system briefly described in the immediately preceding paragraphs. It was a world system that was bringing intense pressures to bear on individuals, families, and religious organizations—particularly those that would not participate in the cult of emperor worship, or who resisted against Roman intrusions into their religious organizations (Crossan 2004, 367). In addition to this pressure, there were also those associated with the Roman economic system with its extremely uneven distribution of resources. There were the extremely rich and the extremely poor, with roughly 10% of Roman officials and aristocrats owning 90% of the world's wealth (Carter 2001, 19; Horsley 2003, 30).

The system involved putting the peasants to work on farms even if given peasants owned them. These products produced the money that was sent to Rome to support the emperor's building projects, military exploits, and/or personal habits. However, the emperor's exploits were so expensive that most peasant families were paying out most of what they produced in taxes, and were barely able to live above survival levels. Moreover, if there were crop failures due to a famine or to some other natural disaster, the amount of taxes owed did not change. Therefore, many families not only lost their homes, but were plunged into poverty, debt bondage, and slavery because they could not pay either the rents or the mortgages on their properties. Large numbers became field hands, wandering from estate to estate seeking work. However, Roman citizens were not directly taxed (Koester 1995, 314). While the vast majority of the population was holding on for dear life, the vast majority was also aware of extravagant building projects such as Nero's Golden House, one of the wonders of the ancient world of that time (Crossan 2004, 124).

Frequently the money received from the peasants was not enough to fund the emperor's projects, so occasionally (Carter 2001, 134), emperors even raided various religious temples for money to fund such projects Temples representing different religions throughout Roman provinces faced this danger constantly, and so did the Jewish temple and synagogues. Sometimes, in addition to raiding the temples, occasionally emperors insisted that statues of themselves be placed alongside those representing gods of various religions (Koester 1995, 303). Sometimes this evoked revolts (379).

At the times of Nero and Domitian, when the book of Revelation is believed to have been composed, these elaborate building projects and other self-ingratiating expenditure of the emperors had reached extremes. Revolts and assassinations were breaking out all over the empire, particularly in Galilee and in the City of Rome. It must have felt like the world was coming apart. Even younger aristocratic Jews, such as first century historian Josephus, who were affiliated with and protected by patronage or family connections, had begun to lend their expertise to revolts from among the peasants. Revolts of revolutionaries such as the Zealots and of terrorist groups such as the Sicarii were escalating (Koester 1995, 381). Again, to the majority of Jews and Christians, it must have seemed as though the world was coming apart.

As mentioned above, it is believed that the author John might have been aware that Nero had executed the apostles Paul, Peter, and James, the brother of Jesus (Crossan 2004, 40). Throughout the period between Nero and Domitian, at various points Jews were expelled from the city of Rome (364), but some had been returning (see Acts 18:2; 364). Just the constant bombardment of news about the saga of the royal family itself would have created a sense of national disturbance. Over this course of time, Nero had murdered several of his family members in order to protect his interests (Koester 1995, 379). Resentment among the Roman Senate and aristocracy was growing, and images of emotional instability of Nero were emerging, including what some scholars believe is an image of Nero as the seven–headed beast in Revelation 13 (Revelation 13:1–18; Koester, 1995, 301; Crossan 2004, 267; Goodman 1997, 56), and rumor had it that Nero was insane.

Then came the event that is believed to have brought the Christian/emperor conflict to a head. It was the fire that destroyed most of the city of Rome (64 C.E.). Rumors circulated that Nero had set the fire (Goodman 1997, 327). To protect his reputation, Nero accused the Christians of setting the fire. That gave him the excuse to round up Christian leaders and murder them. Nero made public displays of Christians, forcing some to clothe themselves in animal skins to be eaten by ravenous dogs. Others were set aflame in order to light public festivals (Ehrman 2003, 420; Crossan 2004, 363). Some believed that the apostle Paul was, by then, in Rome. Based on that, scholars believe that Paul, Peter, and James were among those who were killed at that time (363). At the end of his reign, the emperor whom so many thought was insane committed suicide. The Senate refused to consider Nero a god, as it had most emperors before him, dating all of the way back to Augustus Caesar (Goodman 1997, 230). That is how the Julio–Claudian Dynasty came to an end, and fighting then began over who was to ascend the throne (Ehrman 2003, 466).

When Domitian stepped up to the head of government, conspiracies were already planned against him (81 C.E.). Therefore, it seems that two of the foci of Domitians' reign were to protect himself and to get respect due to a god. The persecution of Christians had to do with their refusal to worship the emperor. Like Nero, Domitian also killed members of his family whom he suspected as being a threat to him (Koester 1995, 300). He demanded to be called "Lord and God." The first epistle of Clement, which is not part of the Bible, but was written around this time, contains graphic details about life and times in periods in which the book of Revelation is believed to have been written. Huge numbers of Christians gave their lives under Nero (Crossan 2004, 400; Ehrman 2003, 168; Ehrman 2004, 453).

Domitian had to continue rebuilding a Rome that had been damaged by the fire that had occurred in Nero's time (Koester 1995, 336). There were intense economic problems associated with raising money to fund various building projects and the military. Like Nero, Domitian engaged in elaborate building projects that had to be funded with a combination of taxing the poor, enforcing slave labor, raiding temples, and confiscating estates from throughout the empire. The last years of Domitian became another reign of terror. He demanded to be called "Lord and God." It was also during this time that other fires broke out in the city of Rome, and that a plague killed a large percentage of the population. Again, this is the bizarre and unstable context in which John, exiled to the Isle of Patmos, began composing the book of Revelation (353). Some scholars believe that, in the book of Revelation, the "Whore of Babylon" is a symbol of the Roman Empire.

Revelation 21 contains an image of a new Heaven and a new Earth where the kingdom of God replaces the evil world system in which the author of Revelation lives. There are many layers to the symbols that are in the book. Throughout Christendom, there have been many interpretations. However, general consensus is that one can begin to understand the various symbols if one begins with the life and times in which the author was living.

The book begins with images of churches that are suffering—suffering due to persecution, false teachings, and apathy (Ehrman 2003, 463). Those who have done what is right will be praised by Christ. Those who have done what is wrong will suffer consequences. Then the remaining of the book describes a series of events that culminate with Satan, the evil force behind the chaos in the evil world system, being thrown into the lake of fire. Death, itself, is also thrown into the lake. It is at that point that the book presents the image of the new Heaven and the new Earth, with features that put Nero's Golden House to shame. The New Jerusalem descends from heaven with streets paved with gold and Christ reigning eternal. It is governed by a new set of principles. Therefore the oppressed can now wipe tears from their eyes (see Revelation 21:4). They can now spend their time in an awesome heavenly worship service, where Jesus Christ and His teachings are the center of attention (see v. 14; 22:1–3; 23). The book ends with the assertion that the vision is true and that it will soon be fulfilled.

It is evident that the author felt that if Christians adopted this vision, they would be able to unify in a spirit of hope and thanksgiving. They could make sense out of what was happening, and they could devote themselves to advancing the kingdom of God on Earth!

BACKGROUND RESEARCH

1. What is to be an ever present feature of God's kingdom on Earth (Revelation 21:1; 2 Peter 3:13)?
2. In your opinion, why is the "New Jerusalem" (God's kingdom) often characterized in Scripture as a virgin (Isaiah 52:1; 2 Corinthians 11:2; Revelation 21:2)?
3. Against the backdrop of the cash crop system being set up wherein peasants paid most of their earnings toward lavish Roman temples for purposes of emperor worship, explain some possible meanings of Revelation 20:3.
4. In a world system that plunged families into poverty, set infants out to die, and divorced and married women for the gain of property, what might the following Scriptures mean: Isaiah 25:8; 1 Corinthians 15:26; Revelation 21:4?
5. How might the author of Revelation 21:4 have been influenced by the following Scriptures in Isaiah 35:10; 51:11; 65:19?
6. In what sense are the images of God in Revelation 21:5 similar to images of God with the Children of Israel in the wilderness (Exodus 17:6; Isaiah 43:19)?

QUESTIONS FOR REVIEW

1. Review the introductory story. What are hints of divisions within the Jefferson family? In what ways might these divisions hint that people see themselves differently than God intended for them to see each other?
2. Compare and contrast the celebration in the introductory story with the one in Revelation 21:1–7.
3. What would be the evidences of the presence of God's kingdom on Earth in the introductory story? Explain.
4. Compare and contrast evidences of God's kingdom advancing on Earth and the stubbornness of the current world system that wars against it. Give concrete examples.
5. What can individuals do to advance God's kingdom on Earth?
6. Ultimately, who is going to win the battle between good and evil? Explain.

RECASTING THE CHARACTERS

1. Outline a family reunion for your family. Where, in the program, would you provide sacred space for the family to envision God working within your family and establishing God's kingdom on Earth?

2. Does your church have family celebrations? How might your church incorporate the celebration of God's work within families within your church extended family?

QUESTION FOR REFLECTION

Does your family and extended family need a spiritually complete makeover? Can you be a catalyst for this change? If so, how? Are there any barriers to this? How can they be handled?

MAKING PEACE VS. MAKING WAR

Rizpah: 2 Samuel 3:7–8; 21:1–14

Meeting at Smitty's barbershop on Thursday afternoon had become a regular Bronzetown neighborhood happening. The hot topic for this particular day was the movie *Hotel Rwanda*. It had been showing at the local theater, and several people had already seen it with their families.

"Them Africans killed a whole bunch of Africans," Macon said. "I ain't never seen nothin' like that."

"I look at it like this," Smitty said. "They keep sayin' the White man could have stopped that. The White man ain't got nothin' to do with that mess. They're just over there killin' each other up. And you expect the White man to go over there and stop 'em? It costs too much money. The White man is gonna keep his money. You know what I'm sayin'?"

"Naw, Smitty," Darius butted in. "It was something else behind that. It must have been something about oil. The United States could have stopped it before it went that far. They have Intelligence that tells them everything that is going on around the world. No, I believe that some big oil company is behind it, trying to get the Blacks to kill each other up so that they can take over the land and build some oil refineries."

"Aw, there you go with another one of those conspiracy theories, Darius," Macon cut in. "But you're wrong this time. It's just like these gangs around here. Every weekend you hear about a Black killin' a Black. When is the last time you saw a White man run down here into these projects and shoot at somebody, huh?"

"But you've got to get the bigger picture, man," said Darius. "Who do you think is supplying the kids with these guns?"

"Yeah, you right," Rufus said, entering the conversation. "You can buy a gun on the street as easy as you can buy a cigarette. And kids have got as many guns as grown people do. Where do you think they're getting 'em?"

"I read somewhere that it's some gun manufacturers that're smugglin' 'em into the neighborhood. They must have some people selling 'em hot," Smitty said.

"Yeah, but who is these 'people' but us? You can't blame everything on the White man," Macon said. "Nobody is forcing us to buy 'em. And nobody is forcing us to shoot at each other, either. We got choices."

"No, no, no," Darius said. "You see, the guns came in with the crack. I read somewhere that when crack entered the central cities, so did the guns. The big drug dealers must be selling guns and crack together. They must be hiring young people to run the drugs. That is where all the killing is coming from. So it isn't just Black people killing Black people. Something else is involved."

"No, Darius," Amos said. "Look at it like this. These gangs have been around here for a long time. They ain't up to no good. No offense, Rufus. I know you are still in one, but we have got to tell it like it is. That's all I'm doing."

"Why are you so hard on the gangs?" Rufus asked. "We do a lot for the neighborhood. And besides, you must be having another memory lapse. I thought I heard you say you once belonged to the Black Panthers. Why you so hard on us, when you once belonged to a gang yourself?"

"Naw, Rufus. You're way off there," Smitty said. "I was a Panther too, but the Panthers weren't anything like these no–count gangs today. We had an agenda and a purpose. We were trying to defend the Black community, not tear it down. We had all kinds of programs for children—"

"You're right about that, Smitty," Amos butted in. "The media said the Panthers was violent, but that's a lie. We wasn't nothing like the gangs today. Gangs today are just doing random violence for no reason. Instead of defending the neighborhood, they're tearin' it up!

And if we don't look out, we'll do a repeat of Hotel Rwanda right here in Bronzetown."

"Yeah, but we do a lot for the neighborhood, too," Rufus countered. "I have employed at least 50 boys right here in the neighborhood. Otherwise they wouldn't have spending money. Some of them use the money to help support their families. Sure, they belong to the gang, and sure they run drugs, and sure they pack a pistol to take care of themselves, but, overall, they are keeping money flowing through the community. Plus we are the only family that some of them know. What would the community do without us?"

"But Rufus, Rufus, Rufus!" Smitty said. "Some of your employees don't know how to handle their business. They get into shoot–outs, and kill innocent people who are just walking down the street or sitting on their porches. They keep the cops coming in and out all the time. They have got the neighborhood on lockdown. The vast majority of people around here are afraid to come out of their homes at night because of these kids, and some of our seniors won't even come out during the day. This is not helping the neighborhood, Rufus. It is keeping the neighborhood on lockdown."

"All of our families are in jeopardy, Rufus," added Darius.

"Shut up, Smitty and Darius," Rufus hollered. "Look down that street there. Here comes Reverend Sampson with his so–called 'Family Neighborhood Self–Help Watch Group.' Here they are marching again and passing out leaflets again. They're a nuisance."

"Looks like he's not gonna stop until he puts these gangs out of business," Smitty said and laughed.

"If you ask me, he's wasting his time," Amos said. "But at least somebody is trying to do something."

"Let me out of here," Rufus yelled, ducking out the back door just as Reverend Sampson crossed the street and moved toward the barber shop.

A CLOSER LOOK

Some men in the introductory story associate what happened in Rwanda with gang warfare in the United States. That might be a stretch, but there are some similarities. There are Black people killing other Black people, based on the group to which they belong. In both cases, there is a struggle for survival. In both, there is a "bigger picture" of political and economic realities that have triggered and are exacerbating the situation.

In both cases, the groups have gone to war rather than choose to resolve their differences through peaceful reconciliation and community building. In both cases, the perpetual state of war continues to threaten the Black families and communities involved as they become more vulnerable to victimization from outside forces (such as drug lords) that do not have the community's well–being as their primary objective. Most significant of all, however, is that both of the groups at war have moved away from basic spiritual values that have traditionally placed God and the celebration of life at the center of community life.

Historians trace the genocide that took place in Rwanda to the struggle for an equal distribution of scarce resources (Meredith 2005, 485). The country had been a colony of Belgium. It had been formed by a combination of Rwanda and Burundi. Belgium had ruled the country through one ethnic group, the Tutsi tribe. With its independence in 1957, a new government had been installed. Part of the responsibility of the new government would be to distribute the resources for the sustenance of African families throughout the country. However, most of the government seats were occupied by Tutsi, with the Hutu tribe occupying very few seats. The Hutu people did not believe that their needs could be adequately considered in such a structure. This situation set the two groups against each other in a bloody civil war. In 1963 alone, an estimated 20,000 Tutsi people were killed in Burundi. In 1988, 50,000 Hutu people fled into Rwanda from Burundi. Then, in 1994, 800,000 Tutsi people and moderate Hutu people were killed over a 100–day period, as two million Hutu people then fled to refugee camps in Zaire (486).

The movie *Hotel Rwanda* provides the details of this tragedy. It is unfortunate that the two groups allowed economic and related political factors to prevent them from deciding for peace, reconciliation, and a plan that would have resulted in the survival of so many African families. Moreover, there does not appear to be any evidence that the people who decided to perform these massacres were in touch with a spirituality that celebrated life and worked against untimely death.

The loss of a spirituality that venerates life and opposes death has also been cited as being at the core of gang violence in the United States. The *Report to Congress on Juvenile Violence Research* revealed that gang violence is most likely to occur in impoverished neighborhoods (Bilchik 1999, 7). Even though it showed that the majority of young people who live in these neighborhoods do not belong to gangs and do not commit violent acts, often a small group of young people in such neighborhoods is responsible for most of the violence that occurs there. For example, the same report found that the majority of such violent crimes took place in the most deprived census tracts of the cities studied (8). The report also noted that over 50% of the crimes occurred in places other than the private residences of the persons committing the crimes. In Los Angeles, for example, 75% of the juvenile homicides were seen to take place in public places such as streets (47%) and automobiles (19%). Twenty–three percent were drive–by shootings (13). In terms of time of day for crimes to occur, the study found that it differed for different cities. In Washington, D.C., for example, during the school year, most shootings took place near schools, at around 3:00 p.m. During the summer, the shootings were most likely to occur between 10:00 p.m. and 2:00 a.m. However, in Milwaukee, 80% of the youth homicides occurred between 4:00 p.m. and 12:00 a.m. Moreover, in Milwaukee, the homicides were also found to be taking place in the most desolate areas of the city (20).

The same study showed that among youth who commit homicides, there were four most frequent motives: gang–related turf or revenge fights, drugs, robberies, and arguments unrelated to gangs. In Los Angeles, for example, an estimated 70% of the violent confrontations were over gang rivalries. Further, 25% of young people surveyed in the study said they knew where to get a gun. Of those who said they owned guns, 70% said they purchased them from a friend. Seven percent said that they knew where they could get a gun within one hour. The most frequent reason that young people in Los Angeles gave for owning a gun was self–defense (Bilchik 1999, 8).

However, researcher Daniel Cork found a link between neighborhood crack activity and gun homicides in the same neighborhoods (Cork 1999, 379). Cork charted how the selling of crack became decentralized and handled through freelancers. He used city–level data on crack arrests and gun related juvenile homicides to document that a dramatic growth in crack cocaine arrests paralleled a dramatic growth in the number of gun homicides committed by youth (379). As the demand for crack escalated, there was a need for more "runners." Heavy penalties for drug trafficking, due to New York's "Rockefeller Laws," led the major drug lords to recruit juveniles as drug runners, because they were not likely to be eligible for prosecution under these laws. Guns became necessary because, being that the trade was being handled outside the law, the drug industry had to develop a policing system that functioned outside the law. Therefore, the threat of carrying out physical violence became a necessary part of the job. Youth found it mandatory to carry guns (383). Cork also found that as crack markets expanded, so did purchases of guns. He cites a Boyum and Kleiman study that found a significant percentage of high school students carrying guns for protection (384). Moreover, this soon involved rival "turf" wars where each gang had a different market and fought to keep rival gangs out of that market (384).

A report entitled *Addressing Community Gang Problems: A Practical Guide* has encouraged neighborhood and community groups such as churches to begin to fight these problems by identifying the reasons that young people join gangs, and how such organizations can provide resources for young people so that they do not feel the need to join gangs and run drugs (Spelman 1998, 67). Rather than focus exclusively on gang violence, churches and community groups are encouraged to set up advisory boards to find out what youth need, and where in the church and community there are resources to meet those needs.

In the case of the church, of course, these needs would include both spiritual and practical necessities such as youth employment or after school programs. This might also involve considering writing grants to outside funding agencies and forming partnerships with such organizations as the Boys and Girls Clubs of America. It may mean fighting on behalf of the parents of such children for legislation regarding the minimum wage, particularly for youth. Another viable suggestion involves partnering with the city administrators to encourage businesses to invest in the areas surrounding the churches (68).

Churches should also consider the fact that it is not uncommon to find children of church members belonging to gangs. It is, therefore, most practical for church educational programs to stress the spiritual values that promote a respect for life and to explain how gang violence and substance abuse are contrary to celebrating God–given life. An example would be stressing how Jesus demonstrated His celebration of life by healing people, bringing people back from the dead, and bringing salvation (see John 3:16). It makes sense that churches give children every opportunity to accept Jesus Christ as Savior. Then churches might offer youth discipleship courses that help children learn to make efficient use of the resources available to them outside of gang networks. This is one of the major ways that the church may be able to restore a healthy respect for life and the celebration of life back to the center of communities now ravaged and "locked down" by senseless homicides and drug trafficking.

A CLOSER LOOK AT RIZPAH
2 Samuel 3:7, 8; 21:1–14

2 Samuel 3:7 Now Saul had had a concubine named Rizpah daughter of Aiah. And Ish-Bosheth said to Abner, "Why did you sleep with my father's concubine?" **8** Abner was very angry because of what Ish-Bosheth said and he answered, "Am I a dog's head—on Judah's side? This very day I am loyal to the house of your father Saul and to his family and friends. I haven't handed you over to David. Yet now you accuse me of an offense involving this woman! **2 Samuel 21:1** During the reign of David, there was a famine for three successive years; so David sought the face of the LORD. The LORD said, "It is on account of Saul and his blood-stained house; it is because he put the Gibeonites to death." **2** The king summoned the Gibeonites and spoke to them. (Now the Gibeonites were not a part of Israel but were survivors of the Amorites; the Israelites had sworn to spare them, but Saul in his zeal for Israel and Judah had tried to annihilate them.) **3** David asked the Gibeonites, "What shall I do for you? How shall I make amends so that you will bless the LORD's inheritance?" **4** The Gibeonites answered him, "We have no right to demand silver or gold from Saul or his family, nor do we have the right to put anyone in Israel to death." "What do you want me to do for you?" David asked. **5** They answered the king, "As for the man who destroyed us and plotted against us so that we have been decimated and have no place anywhere in Israel, **6** let seven of his male descendants be given to us to be killed and exposed before the LORD at Gibeah of Saul—the LORD's chosen one." So the king said, "I will give them to you." **7** The king spared Mephibosheth son of Jonathan, the son of Saul, because of the oath before the LORD between David and Jonathan son of Saul. **8** But the king took Armoni and Mephibosheth, the two sons of Aiah's daughter Rizpah, whom she had borne to Saul, together with the five sons of Saul's daughter Merab, whom she had borne to Adriel son of Barzillai the Meholathite. **9** He handed them over to the Gibeonites, who killed and exposed them on a hill before the LORD. All seven of them fell together; they were put to death during the first days of the harvest, just as the barley harvest was beginning. **10** Rizpah daughter of Aiah took sackcloth and spread it out for herself on a rock. From the beginning of the harvest till the rain poured down from the heavens on the bodies, she did not let the birds of the air touch them by day or the wild animals by night. **11** When David was told what Aiah's daughter Rizpah, Saul's concubine, had done, he went and took the bones of Saul and his son Jonathan from the citizens of Jabesh Gilead. (They had taken them secretly from the public square at Beth Shan, where the Philistines had hung them after they struck Saul down on Gilboa.) **13** David brought the bones of Saul and his son Jonathan from there, and the bones of those who had been killed and exposed were gathered up. **14** They buried the bones of Saul and his son Jonathan in the tomb of Saul's father Kish, at Zela in Benjamin, and did everything the king commanded. After that, God answered prayer in behalf of the land.

Rizpah, in this chapter's Scripture passage, has much in common with Reverend Sampson in the introductory story. Rizpah, too, lives in an environment that has been ravaged by "turf fights." In her case, the warfare is between the forces of Saul, the former king, and the forces of David, who has been installed as the new king. In the chapters leading up to and following the story of Rizpah, there is evidence that this specific turf war is also being waged within a "bigger picture" of socioeconomic realities. The setting of the story is the Late Bronze Age of 1500–1200 B.C.E. (Ceresko 2001, 144).

This would have been a setting in which various major city–states and emerging empires were fighting for trade routes. Egypt would have been at the zenith of its power with influence over Palestine. There was also the Hittite Empire, the Mycean community in Greece, the Minoan community in Crete, and the Maryannu and Mitanni in Northern Mesopotamia, along with the Hurrians. It was a time when the war chariot had been introduced by the Mitanni and this invention had revolutionized how warfare was conducted. Moreover, the Philistines had become masters of the use of iron in the construction of weapons. In fact, the story of Rizpah is in a setting where the most formidable threat of all would have been posed to Israel by the Philistines (Ceresko 2001, 138).

Creating even more chaos would have been the diseases and plaques, which had caused the Israelites' concern for hygiene (see Leviticus 11; Deuteronomy 14:3–21), their avoidance of dead bodies (see Numbers 25) and their care concerning people with whom they interacted (see Joshua 6:21–27). There were also periodic crop failures and famines that were caused by severe changes in weather (Ceresko 2001, 138). In the setting of Rizpah's story, there would have been widespread migrations, economic chaos, and the decline of various civilizations (142).

It was within this general milieu that Saul, David, and Solomon developed a monarchy that lasted for roughly 80 years (Ceresko 2001, 148). However, it was the pressure from the Philistines that had threatened what had been Israelite's federation of tribes, and that had caused the people to want a monarchy for survival. It was the "Sea People" that then would have been threatening Israel's survival as a monarchy. The Philistines threatened not only Israel, but all the neighboring kingdoms and communities as well. No doubt, Israel would have been in a state of desperation at the thought of being taken back into slavery or near slavery, as had been their experience in Egypt (143). In the face of the Philistines, the people of Israel wanted a king because the loosely organized militia units of the tribal confederacy were clearly no match for the Philistine forces (137).

The prophet Samuel had warned the Israelites that pressures of warding off empires such as the Philistines could cause them to depart from basic spiritual values that were at the core of their covenant with God and with each other (see 1 Samuel 18).

When the curtain rises on Rizpah in 2 Samuel 21, she is sitting beside dead bodies on a hill. In the immediately preceding verses, it is plain that a civil war, similar to that of Rwanda, had taken place. It seems that the Gibeonites had become victims of genocide. In order to call a truce, David asked the remaining Gibeonites what they wanted. They responded that killing seven of the sons of Saul would satisfy them. David then offered the children of Saul's concubine, Rizpah, and those of Saul's daughter, Merab. Thus the lives of these children became disrespected and meaningless. In fact, their corpses, along with the corpses of Saul and Jonathan, had not even been given a proper burial. This, of course, showed a horrible disrespect for the dead (see 2 Samuel 21).

Rizpah is seen refusing to leave the bodies of her children and those of the other woman. One can only speculate that she realized that something was terribly wrong in Israel. It is reasonable to consider that she realized the problem was spiritual. No doubt she saw that the celebration of life and the value placed on human beings was a part of the covenant that Israel had with God. She probably understood that this divine covenant was being completely ignored in the interests of establishing "turf" and in the interests of the protection of "honor and shame." However, like Reverend Sampson in the introductory story, she was unwilling to allow things to remain as they were. Even if she was not able to stop the "turf fights" between the forces of Saul and the forces of David, and even if she was unable to bring a cease–fire to the fights between the "Sea People" and Israel, Rizpah was willing to do whatever she could do to stand up for justice and for God.

David, seeing that Rizpah's actions were causing a public relations problem, stopped fighting long enough to attend to the spiritual value of conducting a proper burial for the dead. In essence, this gutsy woman, Rizpah, brought David and all of Israel to its senses—at least for one moment in time.

BACKGROUND RESEARCH

1. Who was Rizpah (2 Samuel 3:7–8)? What might have been one of the ugly realities related to being a concubine?
2. What were some regulations concerning dead bodies in Israel (Genesis 37:34; Job 1:20)?
3. What was traditionally done with bodies before burial (Genesis 50:2–3)?
4. What was remarkable about what Rizpah had done (Leviticus 21:10; 2 Samuel 18:17)?
5. When had David first met a Philistine (1 Samuel 17:4–50)?

QUESTIONS FOR REVIEW

1. What are some differences and similarities between Rizpah and Reverend Sampson in the opening story?
2. What is the "bigger picture" surrounding gang warfare mentioned in the introductory story?
3. What is the implied "bigger picture" in the setting of Rizpah (2 Samuel 3:1–8; 21:1–14)?
4. In contemporary life and the biblical account, what does this "bigger picture" have to do with the murders taking place between people?
5. How does this "bigger picture" impact families today?
6. Are people "bound" by this "bigger picture"? Is there a way out? Explain.
7. Reflect on Reverend Sampson in the introductory story. Are his actions appropriate for a pastor? Explain?
8. Locate at least four Scriptures that celebrate life.

RECASTING THE CHARACTERS

Write Scene II of the introductory story. In this scene, Pastor Sampson is back in his church, and is forming an advisory board that will create a program for youth and parents. The program will provide resources so that young people don't feel the need to join gangs. Pretend that you are on this board. Pretend that you have been asked to identify some Scriptures, biblical examples, examples from African American history, and other sources as stimuli for discussion about the spiritual component of such a program. Create bullet points that suggest what you would bring to the next advisory board meeting.

QUESTION FOR REFLECTION

In what ways might the content of this chapter relate to your life and/or the lives of your family members, both immediate and extended?

REPAIRING VS. DISRUPTING

Rebuilding God's Holy Places: Ezra 1:1–8; 2:1–2, 62–70; 3:1–2, 7, 10–13; Isaiah 40:1–14

For many former residents of New Orleans, the date August 28, 2005, will always be remembered as one of the most traumatic days of their lives. It was the date that Hurricane Katrina forced thousands of people to vacate their homes and relocate to other cities throughout the country. Most will recall that, by the end of that year, Mayor Nagin was inviting people to return and help rebuild the city. However, the question that was by then being debated on radio talk shows, in online discussion groups, and in newspaper editorials throughout the country was whether, in fact, people should return to New Orleans and whether the city actually should be rebuilt. Following are paraphrases of comments from some Internet discussion groups that reveal how both the general public and evacuees were divided in their opinions:

"Yes! Emphatically! New Orleans is worth rebuilding! The cuisine, the music, the history, the architecture, and the people are all worth bringing back! We can rebuild, solidify, and improve the levees. The original residents need to return, live, work, and be safe from future hurricanes."

"It is true that New Orleans has a rich history, but now that the city has been destroyed, it is time to leave it and move on. Why go back there with a false sense of hope?"

"Going back and investing in New Orleans would be like investing in one of the Fortune 500 companies that recently went under. Why get hit twice? It'll never be the same anyway, regardless of how much money the government puts into it."

"I want the city to be rebuilt! I want to go home. I am from the 9th Ward of New Orleans, and most of my family lives there. Not rebuilding this wonderful city would be an insult to people who are already suffering from being away from home. I want to be home by Christmas of next year. I am optimistic."

"We should rebuild it so that the original neighborhoods look the same. New Orleans is a national treasure. We must be mindful of its historical and architectural integrity. That must be preserved and respected."

"One's soul is anchored in one's hometown. This is true of the millions of people who lived here. We move forward by rebuilding. That is how we care about one another. We must find ways to support one another as we rebuild."

"No! Let's respect God's plan. God wanted this area to stand as a buffer between the land and the ocean. Let God reclaim the swamp and just let the people relocate elsewhere to a safer environment."

"I agree. It was the will of God. New Orleans needs to repent and turn back to God. They were warned of God's judgment and they did not wake up. If they do not repent, it will just happen all over again."

"Oh, come on! If it was because of sin, every city in America should be hit. The whole country is like Sodom and Gomorrah, baby! No! Why not just use the best of technology to repair the place so that the people can return to their homes?"

"God ain't had nothin' to do with that! That happened because they didn't fix those levees when they was supposed to! They didn't care because the people was Black. If you ask me, it's a case of racism. God ain't had nothin' to do with that."

"Restoration is virtually impossible, plus the magic cannot be rebuilt. It would be a cheap imitation."

"It doesn't make any sense to spend money rebuilding this city. The weather conditions won't go away. All that will happen is that people will be hurt again. I would rather make a better life in a safer place."

"When has America ever backed away from nature? Of course it should be rebuilt—so that people can have as much protection as possible."

"It would be nice to see how we could use all of the latest technology to rebuild the city, but the truth is, it won't work. We should just chalk this up to experience. Learn from it so that we can be ready for the next disaster, but we should not go back."
(CNN.com 10/3/05)

A CLOSER LOOK

Hurricane Katrina left the city of New Orleans devastated. After an estimated 400,000 people had to evacuate, most of the city appeared like a ghost town. While the 2000 United States Census had estimated that 213,000 homes were in New Orleans, Mayor Ray Nagin had reported that over 80% of them had been flooded (Almasy 2005). Moreover, the Louisiana Department of Environmental Quality estimated that between 140,000 and 160,000 homes needed to be leveled, and more than 350,000 vehicles were ruined (Almasy 2005). The 9th Ward was where most of the poorest among African American residents of the city had lived. It was the ward that was closest to the levees that broke, and it was the ward that was the most devastated, remaining practically below sea level.

Between August 28, when the hurricane struck, and mid–November, the city went from a thriving tourist attraction to nearly a ghost town, inhabited mostly by male laborers, contractors, security guards, and police agencies, scoping out the city to determine whether, and/or how the city could be rebuilt (CNN.com 10/4/05). By the end of the year, most of the television cameras had left New Orleans (Grassi 2005). Some residents had either remained to wait out the storm, or had left and then gradually made their way back into the city. Newspapers were quoting them as saying they did not have jobs, and the social services that they had been able to locate were soon becoming depleted. In late October, the mayor of the city had announced that they did not have the money to continue funding 3,000 civilian government jobs. The city had gone bankrupt, with its future financial state uncertain (Grassi 2005).

As late as November, two thousand prisoners were still being held on minor offenses in Angola, a notorious former slave plantation of rural Louisiana, and their plight had yet to become a local priority. In fact, chances were that their records had been washed away in the flood, and no one had offered a solution to the problem (CNN.com 10/7/05). By year–end, a small trickle of Latino immigrants were slowly making their way into the city to do reconstruction in very dangerous conditions, for low pay, and with no medical care. Some had already become ill (Flaherty 2005).

Worse yet, by November, landlords had been found placing eviction notices on the homes of people who had vacated the city. Deals were being made to level their homes and build new ones that could be rented and sold for higher prices than these people would be able to pay (Flaherty 2005). This situation had opened up the debate over whether, in fact, New Orleans was being rebuilt for the rich. The question was being asked whether the renovation plans would incorporate safety nets for the poor and working socioeconomic groups (Harden 2005).

What was also being considered is that, by December 2005, the vast majority of New Orleans evacuees had resettled into other communities. The news media reported varying degrees of success in the evacuees locating lost relatives, finding employment, and enrolling children into new schools. As the previous online discussion reveals, these resettled evacuees were divided in their opinions as to whether to return to the city.

Yet, what is phenomenal is that the media also carried images of African American families who, in the midst of the chaos, were still praising God and remaining hopeful. One example is the story of six members of one extended family who had to be relocated all the way to Massachusetts. The family members spanned three generations and were all living together in an evacuation center. One person, of this same family, in his 30's, had to learn to share a barracks with his brother, who was eight years younger than him. However, this man was quoted as telling the Christian Science Monitor reporter, "It's all good. It's all good." Instead of sharing in customary dinners at the family matriarch's home, they found themselves having to create a new family ritual. At the same time every day, they took their places in the food line. Then they gathered together at vacant spots on tables, pulling up chairs, with some sitting on floors. They bowed their heads and thanked God in the midst of it all (Teicher 2005).

In spite of the strangeness of the entire situation, Connie, the matriarch of the family, was quoted as telling a reporter that this was what she had of her family for now, and she was going to be thankful. She was exhibiting three of the values that Joyce Ladner identified as timeless in the African American family tradition: the "Can–Do" spirit, "Make a Way Out of No Way," and "Trust in the Lord" (Ladner 1998, 119).

In another story, three young men had to be relocated from New Orleans to Austin, Texas, into a mostly White community, where they would attend a mostly White high school. In their previous school, they were drum majors and belonged to a band that emulated the bands at historically Black colleges such as Southern and Grambling State. However, the high school where they were attending emulated the University of Texas! Yet, these three young men, who had never met before, bonded and created a sense of "family" in the midst of what might otherwise have been chaos (Buchholz 2005). They were exhibiting African American values that Joyce Ladner has identified as "Stand Tall" and "Make a Way Out of No Way" (Ladner 1998, 99).

Moreover, in the midst of the online debates, one could notice still other voices, thanking God, praising God, and remaining hopeful:

"It's a miracle! I just got word that my three missing loved ones have been found! My mother is very ill and she made it. Don't give up on hope! Don't give up on God! I also have two sisters who have been found. Never give up!"

"I would like to share a miracle with you in this time of tragedy. My mother made it out of the city alive. She had said, after the levee broke, that black water had come all the way up to the second floor. Then another citizen came by on a boat and took her to her vehicle that was on a higher ground. She made her way to Interstate 10 and drove to Baton Rouge. She has lost everything but her life, but praise God for that. She is happy to be alive."

"When I realized that the storm was coming, I called to tell my daughter and grandchildren to leave, but at first they wouldn't. They had left because of the previous two hurricanes, so they didn't want to leave again. Then I got a message on my answering machine that my daughter had made it to a church, even though she had lost everything. My daughter called me later to tell me that the water had rushed into their apartment and they had almost drowned. They had to break into a church to save their lives. I thanked God that the church was there!"
(CNN 10/11/2005)

Throughout the discussions that took place, it was clear that everyone understood that the devastation that took place in New Orleans was not entirely due to Hurricane Katrina. It was fully understood that the fact that the levees broke is what caused the major devastation, particularly in the 9th Ward where most of the Black people lived. Yet, the question that kept being raised was whether the levees broke because the people in the 9th Ward had sinned, or whether they broke because the people who were supposed to repair them had sinned by being neglectful? Was this a cause of the people getting what they deserved, or was it a case of man's inhumanity to man?

A similar type of debate was going on among the Israelites as they returned to Judah after the Babylonian Exile.

A CLOSER LOOK AT REBUILDING GOD'S HOLY PLACES
Ezra 1:1–8; 2:1–2, 62–70; 3:1–2, 7, 10–13; Isaiah 40:1–14

Ezra 1:1 In the first year of Cyrus king of Persia, in order to fulfill the word of the LORD spoken by Jeremiah, the LORD moved the heart of Cyrus king of Persia to make a proclamation throughout his realm and to put it in writing: **2** "This is what Cyrus king of Persia says: "'The LORD, the God of heaven, has given me all the kingdoms of the earth and he has appointed me to build a temple for him at Jerusalem in Judah. **3** Anyone of his people among you—may his God be with him, and let him go up to Jerusalem in Judah and build the temple of the LORD, the God of Israel, the God who is in Jerusalem. **4** And the people of any place where survivors may now be living are to provide him with silver and gold, with goods and livestock, and with freewill offerings for the temple of God in Jerusalem.'" **5** Then the family heads of Judah and Benjamin, and the priests and Levites—everyone whose heart God had moved—prepared to go up and build the house of the LORD in Jerusalem. **6** All their neighbors assisted them with articles of silver and gold, with goods and livestock, and with valuable gifts, in addition to all the freewill offerings. **7** Moreover, King Cyrus brought out the articles belonging to the temple of the LORD, which Nebuchadnezzar had carried away from Jerusalem and had placed in the temple of his god. **8** Cyrus king of Persia had them brought by Mithredath the treasurer, who counted them out to Sheshbazzar the prince of Judah. (See also Ezra 2:1–2, 62–70; 3:1–2, 7, 10–13; Isaiah 40:1–14.)

There are both striking similarities and striking differences between the evacuees from New Orleans and the people whose ancestors had been banished from their homelands in Judah. In the New Orleans instance, the precipitating factor was a hurricane and the breaking of the levees. In the Israelite example, it was political exile. Biblical scholars estimate that as many as 20,000 people were driven out of Judah. This is based on figures from Jeremiah 52:28 (a figure that only includes mature men), multiplied by four (to account for the families of the men) (Smith 1991, 73).

Among the evacuees from New Orleans and among the victims of the Babylonian Exile, there were no doubt people who were divided in their opinions about why these tragedies had happened, and whether they were to return to their homelands. In both cases, the land to which they were returning had been devastated, and there were reservations about the practicality of trying to restore it. In both examples, the original residents had been scattered throughout a diaspora. In the circumstances surrounding the New Orleans residents, the diaspora was all over the United States. For Israel, it was all over the Ancient Near East and Africa. In both events, some people chose to remain in their places of relocation.

However, the most striking similarity between the two groups is the evidence that, for large numbers of families, a key resource for resilience (bouncing back) was their ability to hold onto timeless spiritual values that had become deeply ingrained in their respective cultures. In both situations, the people were able to recall the activities of God in their respective histories, and this history became a resource for rejuvenation. In the case of the Israelites, their key resiliency factor was their ability to recall God's covenant, the history of how God had delivered them from slavery in Egypt and their ability to recall the prophecies that contained visions of their future deliverance (see Isaiah 40:1–14).

In the case of African Americans, this is consistent with the five key strengths of African American families, as identified by Dr. Robert Hill: strong kinship bonds, a strong work orientation, an adaptability of family roles, a high achievement orientation, and a strong religious orientation (Hill 2003, i). These values have become apparent in one story after another of New Orleans evacuees struggling to reconstitute themselves and their families, as they have either adapted to their new environments or have attempted to return to New Orleans. Parallel themes have been found among the Israelites as expressed in the prophecies they had been reviewing during their stay in Babylon (see Isaiah 40–55).

However, by the time of Cyrus' edict, there were more Jews living outside Judah than in Judah (Ceresko 2001, 257). In fact, among the people in Diaspora, there were many more people who had actually been born in the lands to which their ancestors had been banished, than there were who had been among the original exiles. The crowd that had returned to Judah was multigenerational (271). Additionally, there were very few people living in Judah who were alive at the time of the Babylonian Exile. Most of those in Judah at the time that the people were returning, in response to Cyrus' edict, were grandchildren and great–grandchildren of people who were alive at the time of the beginning of the Exile (Smith 1991, 73).

Moreover, there were many critical differences between the people whose ancestors had remained in Judah and those whose ancestors had lived in Babylon. Some were economic and some were religious. For example, those who had been banished by Nebuchadnezzar had been mostly aristocrats with skills that could be used in Babylon (Ceresko 2001, 242). Those who had been left behind were mostly people who either worked at lower levels of various government organizations or businesses, or they were peasants. Some of the aristocrats were soon to be commissioned by the Persians to be the indigenous administrators of Judah. They would become part of a complex administrative structure that would last all of the way down to the invasion of Alexander the Great in 333

B.C. This, of course, would lead to conflict between the wealthy and the poor, just as it had been predicted to occur in the course of the reconstruction of New Orleans. The conflicts arose over the distribution of resources (Harden 2005).

Biblical scholars have noted that another likely source of conflict would have been differences in the way that the Hebrew Bible (mainly the Torah) was being interpreted. There would also have been differences in opinion as to the importance of obeying certain parts of the Law, as well as what they perceived to be the consequences of not obeying these parts of the law (see Nehemiah 13:23–27). These conflicts would have been mostly between those who had lived where there was a temple (as in Jerusalem) and those who had lived in a land where there was no temple (Ceresko 2001, 69).

Similar to the conflicts that would develop over ownership of property by New Orleans evacuees, conflicts naturally developed between Jews who had remained in Judah, those who were returning, and people who had been considered outsiders. Mostly this involved disputes over land. Some of the returning Jews were, of course, interested in gaining back the land that their ancestors had once had, but those lands might have already been taken by the people whose ancestors had remained in Judah (see Nehemiah 4).

Of course, the major problem facing everyone was the condition of the land. It had not been recovered since the original Exile. As in the case of the returnees to New Orleans, the people realized that recovery would be slow and would require cooperation from everyone involved. The question on everyone's mind was the need for resources to rebuild (see Ezra 1:5–11).

As the drama of how these Jews "got over" begins to unfold one more time, one can see the people once again combining their resources and refocusing on their covenant with God as central to their lives. We can see them again reorganizing based on community principles that had been the previous basis of their loose federation of tribes, before Israel became a monarchy. Once again, they attempted to rebuild their families for the new situations in which they found themselves (see Ezra 2). It was also a time when the community was desperately trying to make sense out of the suffering that had taken place. It was during this time that some scholars believe that the story of Job might have been written down and rehearsed over and over again (see Job 1–3). It is easy to imagine a group of elders, bent over a scroll containing the story of Job, using the story to draw conclusions about some of their situations. There might have been some debate among them that was parallel to the debates between Job and his three friends (see Job 2:11–13). Was what had happened to them really due to sin, or was it mostly due to man's (represented by Babylon, in this instance) inhumanity to man?

BACKGROUND RESEARCH

1. How did the people go about organizing themselves after they returned to Judah? How important was the extended family (Ezra 2; Nehemiah 7)?
2. How did the returning exiles describe the results of their situation during the period of exile and the impact it had on their families (Ezra 9:1–2)?
3. What role did spirituality and repentance play in the way the returning exiles saw themselves (Ezra 10:2–4, 10–12; Isaiah 61:6–8)?
4. What were some of the characteristics of people who had been left in Judah during the Babylonian Exile (Jeremiah 40)?
5. Who are some people, besides the Jews, who might have owned land in Judah when the exiles returned (1 Kings 8:33; Deuteronomy 28:43)?
6. How might the reading of Ezekiel 11:14–18 have influenced the way that the exiles approached their return to Judah?
7. How might their reflecting on the words of the prophet Jeremiah have influenced how they felt about returning to Judah (Jeremiah 32:6–15)?
8. How might the poor farmers who had remained in Judah have felt about the returning aristocrats and about the government, in general (Nehemiah 5)?
9. Read Job 1–3. Was Job's tragedy due to sin?

QUESTIONS FOR REVIEW

1. Review the introductory story. Contrast the opinions of those who believe that New Orleans should be rebuilt with those who do not believe that it should be. What are their key points of contrast?
2. Review the passages from Ezra listed at the beginning of this chapter. Contrast the opinions of those who are excited about returning to Judah, and those who might be ambivalent. What are the key points of contrast?
3. What are some similarities between the evacuees of New Orleans and the Jews who were returning to Judah from the Babylonian Exile.
4. In your opinion, what is the most outstanding difference between the tragedy of what happened in New Orleans and what happened in the case of the Babylonian Exile?

5. What is one source of courage that the Israelites brought with them from exile (Isaiah 40:1–11)? What about this passage is so encouraging?
6. Review the passages from Ezra. Match verses with each of the following strengths that Robert Hill has identified, thousands of years later, among strong African Americans: strong kinship bonds, strong work orientation, adaptability of family roles, high achievement orientation, and strong religious orientation.

RECASTING THE CHARACTERS

Review the online discussion that took place concerning New Orleans. Select at least three remarks, and respond to them. Select at least one response to which you can respond with passages from the Bible.

QUESTION FOR REFLECTION

What are some messages from Isaiah 40:1–11 that can be shared with someone who has experienced a tragedy? Put the messages in your own words. How does this passage apply to your life?

BIBLIOGRAPHY

Akbar, Naim. "Nigrescence and Identity: Some Limitations." *Counseling Psychologist* 17, no. 2 (1989): 258–303.

Algaze, Guillermo. *The Uruk World System: The Dynamics of Expansion of Early Mesopotamian Civilization*. Chicago: University of Chicago Press, 1993.

Almasy, Steve. "New Orleans to Rebuild Amid Uncertainty." CNN.*com*, 4 October 2005. http://www.cnn.com/2005/US/10/03/new.orleans.rebuilding/index.html

Altschul, Paisius, ed. *An Unbroken Circle: Linking Ancient African Christianity to the African–American Experience*. St. Louis, Mo.: Brotherhood of St. Moses the Black, 1997.

AreaConnect. "Detroit MI Crime Statistics (2004 Crime Data.)" *Detroit Michigan Crime Statistics and Data Resources*. http://detroit.areaconnect.com/crime1.htm

Barnhill, Sandra. "Three Generations at Risk: Imprisoned Women, Their Children and Grandmother Caregivers." *Generations* 20 (Spring 1996): 39–40.

Benson, Peter L., and Michael Donahue. "Ten–Year Trends: At Risk Behaviors." *Journal of Adolescent Research* 4, no. 2 (1989): 125–129.

Bilchik, Shay. *Report to Congress on Juvenile Violence Research*. Report. Washington, D.C.: Office of Juvenile Justice and Delinquency Prevention, 1999. http://www.ncjrs.gov/pdffiles1/176976.pdf

Billingsley, Andrew. *Climbing Jacob's Ladder: The Enduring Legacy of African–American Families*. New York: Touchstone, 1992.

————.*Mighty Like A River: The Black Church and Social Reform*. New York: Oxford University Press, 1999.

Birchett, Colleen. *God's Power to Help Hurting People*. Chicago: Urban Ministries, 2003.

————.*How I Got Over*. Chicago: Urban Ministries, 1993.

————.*Lean On Me*. Nashville: United Methodist Publishing House, 2003.

————.*Real World Christians*. Nashville: United Methodist Publishing House, 2002.

Birchett, Colleen, and Jay Godfrey. "The Darfur Crisis in the Sudan." *United Methodist Seminars on National and International Affairs Newsletter* 6 (Fall 2005).

Bixler, Mark. *The Lost Boys of Sudan: An American Story of the Refugee Experience*. Athens, Ga.: University of Georgia Press, 2005.

Boswell, John. *The Kindness of Strangers: The Abandonment of Children in Western Europe from Late Antiquity to the Renaissance*. New York: Random House Trade, 1988.

Boyd–Franklin, Nancy. *Black Families in Therapy: Understanding the African American Experience*. New York: The Guilford Press, 2003.

Broder, John M., and Dean E. Murphy. "Storm and Crisis: Neighbor States; Houston Struggles to Keep Up with a Surge of Evacuees Estimated at 200,000." *The New York Times*, 3 September 2005. http://select.nytimes.com/gst/abstract.html?res=FB0D1EFA3F550C708C DDA00894DD404482&n=Top%2fReference%2fTimes%20Topics%2fPeopl e%2fR%2fRahimi%2c%20Shadi

Buchholz, Brad. "Finding a New Beat." *Austin American–Statesman*, 6 November 2005.

Burton, Linda. "Age Norms, The Timing of Family Role Transitions and Intergenerational Caregiving Among Aging African American Women." *Gerontologist* 36, no. 2 (1996): 199–208.

————. "Black Grandparents Rearing Children of Drug–Addicted Parents: Stressors, Outcomes, and Social Service Needs." *Gerontologist* 32, no. 6 (1992): 744.

Cadwallader, Tom W., and Robert B. Cairns. "Developmental Influences and Gang Awareness Among African American Inner City Youth." *Social Development* 11, no. 2 (2002): 245–265.

Carr, David. "Canonization in the Context of Community: An Outline of the Formation of the Tanakh and the Christian Bible." A *Gift of God in Due Season: Essays on Scripture and Community in Honor of James* A. *Sanders*. Edited by Richard D. Weis. New York: Sheffield Academic Press, 1996, 22–63.

————. "Controversy and Convergence in Recent Studies of the Formation of the Pentateuch." *Religious Studies Review* 23, no. 1 (1997): 22–32.

————."Synergy Toward Life: A Paradigm for Liberative Christian Work with the Bible." *Quarterly Review* 10, no. 4 (1990): 40–58.

Carruthers, Iva, Frederick D. Haynes III, and Jeremiah A. Wright Jr. eds. B*low the Trumpet in Zion!: Global Vision and Action for the 21st–century Black Church.* Minneapolis: Augsburg Fortress Publishers, 2005.

Carter, Matthew. *Matthew and Empire: Initial Explorations*. Harrisburg, Pa.: Trinity Press International, 2001.

Ceresko, Anthony R. *Introduction to the Old Testament: A Liberation Perspective*. Maryknoll, N.Y.: Orbis Books, 2001.

Chase–Lansdale, P. Lindsay, Jeanne Brooks–Gunn, and Elise S. Zamsky. "Young African–American Multigenerational Families in Poverty: Quality of Mothering and Grandmothering." Edited by Aletha Huston, Vonnie McLoyd, and Cynthia Garcial–Coll. *Child Development, Special Issue: Children and Poverty* 65, no. 2 (1994): 373–393.

Children's Defense Fund Action Council. *Stand Up For Children Now: State of America's Children Action Guide*. Washington, D.C.: Children's Defense Fund Action Council, 2005.

Christian, Marcelle D., and Oscar A. Barbarian. "Cultural Resources and Psychological Adjustment of African American Children: Effects of

Spirituality and Racial Attribution." *Journal of Black Psychology* 27, no. 1 (2001): 43–63.

Clifford, Richard J. "Second Isaiah." *Interpreters Dictionary of the Bible*. Edited by Keith R. Crim and George A. Buttrick. Nashville, Tenn.: Abingdon Press, 1976.

CNN. "New Orleans to Rebuild Amid Uncertainty." CNN.*com*, 4 October 2005. http://www.cnn.com/2005/US/10//03/new.orleans.rebuilding/index.html

————."Web site Hopes to Reunite Katrina Kids with Parents." CNN.*com*, 5 September 2005. http://www.cnn.com/2005/TECH/internet/09/05/allen/index.html

————."Your e–mails: Rebuild New Orleans?" CNN.*com*, 3 October 2005. http://www.cnn.com/2005/US/10/03/feedback.rebuild/index.html

————."Your e–mails: Rebuild New Orleans?" CNN.*com*, 7 October 2005. http://www.cnn.com/2005/US/10/04/feedback.rebuild.a/index.html

————."Your e–mails: The Spirit of New Orleans. CNN.*com*, 11 October 2005. http://www.cnn.com/2005/US/10/10/feedback.spirit/index.html

Cohen, Cathy, J. "Service Provider or Policymaker? Black Churches and Health of African Americans." In *Long March Ahead: African American Churches and Public Policy in Post–civil Rights America* (*Public Influences of African American Churches*). Edited by R. Drew Smith. Durham, N.C.: Duke University Press, 2004.

Cole, Harriette, and John Pinderhughes. *Coming Together: Celebrations for African American Families*. New York: Jump at the Sun Hyperion Books for Children, 2003.

Collins, Patricia Hill. *Black Feminist Thought: Knowledge, Consciousness, and the Politics of Empowerment*. New York: Routledge, 2000.

Cork, Daniel. "Examining Space–Time Interaction in City–Level Homicide Data: Crack Markets and the Diffusion of Guns Among Youth." *Journal of Quantitative Criminology*, 15, no. 4, (1999).

Cosby, Camille O., and Renee Poussaint, eds. *Legendary African American Elders Speak: A Wealth of Wisdom.* New York: Atria Books, 2004.

Cowan, Alison Leigh, Susan Saulny, and Peter C. Beller. "Storm and Crisis: Havens; Airlift of Evacuees to Northeast Is Under Way." *The New York Times,* 9 September 2005.
http://query.nytimes.com/gst/fullpage.html?res=9A04E0DD1331F93AA3
575AC0A9639C8B63&n=Top%2fReference%2fTimes%20Topics%2fPeopl
e%2fS%2fSaulny%2c%20Susan

Cox, Carole B. "Empowering African American Custodial Grandparents." *Social Work* 47, no. 1 (2002): 45–54.

Crenshaw, James L. *Old Testament: Story and Faith: A Literary and Theological Introduction.* Peabody, Mass.: Hendrickson Publishers, 1992.

Crossan, John Dominic. *Jesus: A Revolutionary Biography.* New York: HarperCollins, 1994.

Crossan, John Dominic, and Jonathan L. Reed. *Excavating Jesus: Beneath the Stones, Behind the Texts.* New York: HarperSanFrancisco, 2001.

————.*In Search of Paul: How Jesus' Apostle Opposed Rome's Empire with God's Kingdom.* New York: HarperSanFrancisco, 2004.

Du Bois, W. E. B. *The Souls of Black Folk.* New York: Penguin Classics, 1989.

————.*Black Reconstruction.* New York: Free Press, 1998.

Dunaway, Wilma A. *The African American Family in Slavery and Emancipation.* New York: Cambridge University Press, 2003.

Edersheim, Alfred. *The Life and Times of Jesus the Messiah.* Peabody, Mass.: Hendrickson Publishers, 1993.

Ehrman, Bart D. *Lost Scriptures: Books That Did Not Make It Into the New Testament.* New York: Oxford University Press, 2003.

————.*The New Testament: A Historical Introduction to the Early Christian Writings.* New York: Oxford University Press, 2004.

Ferguson, Everett. *Backgrounds of Early Christianity.* Grand Rapids, Mich.: Eerdmans, 1993.

Fiore, B. "Cynicism and Skepticism." In *Dictionary of New Testament Background.* Edited by Craig A. Evans and Stanley E. Porter. Downers Grove, Ill.: InterVarsity Press, 2000.

Fitzpatrick, Lisa, Eugene McCray, and Dawn K. Smith. "The Global HIV/AIDS Epidemic and Related Mental Health Issues: The Crisis for Americans and Black Americans." *Journal of Black Psychology* 30, no. 1 (2004): 11–23.

Flaherty, Jordan. "Changing New Orleans." ZNET, 6 November 2005. http://www.zmag.org/content/showarticle.cfm?SectionID=72&ItemID=9061

Foster, Herbert J. "African Patterns in the Afro–American Family." *Journal of Black Studies* 14, no. 2 (1983): 201–232.

Freyne, Sean. *Galilee: From Alexander the Great to Hadrian, 323 BCE to 135 CE: A Study of Second Temple Judaism.* Notre Dame, Ind.: University of Notre Dame, 1980.

Garland, David, ed. *Mass Imprisonment: Social Causes and Consequences.* Thousand Oaks, Calif.: Sage Publications, 2001.

Gibson, Priscilla A. "African American Grandmothers as Caregivers: Answering the Call to Help Their Grandchildren." *Families in Society* 83, no.1 (2002): 35–43.

————."Caregiving Role Affects Family Relationship of African American Grandmothers as New Mothers Again: a Phenomenological Perspective." Journal of Marital and Family Therapy 28 (July 2002): 341–353.

Goffe, Leslie. "Sudan's 'Lost Boys' in America." BBC News, 31 August 2004. http://news.bbc.co.uk/2/hi/africa/3602724.stm

Goldman, Benjamin. *Toxic Waste and Race.* New York: United Church of Christ Commission, 1987, p. 7.

Goodman, Martin. *The Roman World* 44 B.C.–A.D. 180 (*Routledge History of the Ancient World*). New York: Routledge, 1997.

Gottwald, Norman. *The Hebrew Bible in its Social World and in Ours*. Atlanta: Scholars Press, 1993.

————.*The Tribes of Yahweh*: A Sociology of the Religion of Liberated Israel, 1250–1050 BCE. New York: Sheffield Press, 1999.

Grassi, Diane M. "Return of New Orleans' Displaced, No Easy Task." OpinionEditorials.com, 6 November 2005. http://www.opinioneditorials.com/guestcontributors/dgrassi_20051106.html

Griffin, Miriam T. *Nero: The End of a Dynasty*. London: B. T. Batsford, 1984.

Haight, Wendy L. *African–American Children at Church*. New York: Cambridge University Press, 2002.

Harden, Blaine. "The Economics of Return: Class, Color May Guide Repopulation of New Orleans." *The Washington Post*, 19 October 2005, A.

Harper, M.S., and Alexander, C.E. "Profile of the Black Elderly." In *Minority Aging: Essential Curricula Content for Selected Health and Allied Professions*. Edited by Mary Harper. Rockville, Md.: U.S. Department of Health and Human Services, 1990.

Hill, Robert. *The Strengths of Black Families*. Lanham, Md.: University Press of America, 2003.

Hoge, Warren. "U.N. Charges Sudan Ignores Rapes in Darfur by Military and Police." *The New York Times*, 30 July 2005, A8. http://select.nytimes.com/gst/abstract.html?res=FA0A13FA3A5B0C738FDDAE0894DD404482

Hopkins, Dwight. *Black Theology of Liberation*. Maryknoll, N.Y.: Orbis Books, 2004.

————.*Down, Up, and Over: Slave Religion and Black Theology*. Minneapolis, Minn.: Augsburg Fortress Publishers, 1999.

Horsley, Richard A. *Jesus and Empire: The Kingdom of God and the New World Disorder*. Minneapolis, Minn.: Augsburg Fortress Publishers, 2003.

Horsley, Richard A., ed. *Paul and Empire: Religion and Power in Roman Imperial Society*. Harrisburg, Pa.: Trinity Press International, 1997.

————.*Paul and the Roman Imperial Order*. Harrisburg, Pa.: Trinity Press International, 2004.

Jarrett, Robin. "African American Mothers and Grandmothers in Poverty: An Adaptational Perspective." *Journal of Comparative Family Studies* 2, no. 9 (1998): 387–396.
————."Growing Up Poor: The Family Experiences of Socially Mobile Youth in Low–Income African American Neighborhoods." *Journal of Adolescent Research* 10, no.1 (1995): 111–125.

Jeremias, Joachim. *Jerusalem in the Time of Jesus: An Investigation into Economic and Social Conditions During the New Testament Period*. Minneapolis, Minn.: Fortress Press, 1969.

Joffrey, Norman. "Political Economy in Early Mesopotamian States." *Annual Review of Anthropology* 24 (1995): 281.

Johnson, Byron, Jung Joon Jang, Spencer De Li, and David Larson. "The Invisible Institution and Black Youth Crime: The Church as an Agency of Local Social Control." *Journal of Youth and Adolescence* 29, no. 4 (2000).

Josephus, Flavius. *The Works of Josephus*. Translated by William Whiston. Peabody, Mass.: Hendrickson Publishers, 1980.

Koester, Helmut. *History, Culture, and Religion of the Hellenistic Age. Introduction to the New Testament, Volume I*. New York: Walter de Gruyter Press, 1987.

Kooy, V. H. "First–born." In *The Interpreters Dictionary of the Bible* (5 Volume Set). Edited by Keith R. Crim and George A. Buttrick. Nashville, Tenn.: Abingdon Press, 1976.

Kraemer, Ross S. "Jewish Mothers and Daughters in the Greco–Roman World." In *The Jewish Family in Antiquity*. Edited by Shaye J. D. Cohen. Atlanta, Ga.: Scholars Press; Brown Judaic Studies, 1993.

Kunjufu, Jawanza. *Adam! Where Are You? Why Most Black Men Don't Go to Church*. Chicago: African American Images, 1994.

Lacey, Marc. "Chaos Grows in Darfur Conflict as Militias Turn on Government." *The New York Times*. 18 October 2005, 1, A1. http://sclect.nytimes.com/gst/abstract.html?res=FA0E14FB3E5B0C7B8 DDDA90994DD404482
———."Rebels' Split Said to Threaten Darfur Peace." *The New York Times*. 7 October 2005. http://www.nytimes.com/glogin?URI=http://www.nytimes.com/2005/10/07/international/africa/07sudan–brief.html&OQ=_rQ3D1&OP=66aabc9 1Q2F6ayE6UkZtQ25kkXq6qQ7DQ7DB6vQ7D6Q7DF6Q235XyQ255uXQ2 3k5u46usQ25Q23Zu6Q7DFtYUu5Q24EQ25Q23ysQ3DzXd4

Ladner, Joyce A. *The Ties that Bind: Timeless Values for African American Families*. New York: John Wiley and Sons, 1998.

Lee, Bernard J. *The Galilean Jewishness of Jesus: Retrieving the Jewish Origins of Christianity (Conversation on the Road not Taken Volume 2)*. Mahwah, N.J.: Paulist Press, 1988.

Lewis, T. "First–born." In *The Interpreter's Dictionary of the Bible* (5 Volume Set). Edited by Keith R. Crim and George A. Buttrick. Nashville, Tenn.: Abingdon Press, 1976.

Li, Xiaoming, Bonita Stanton, Robert Pack, Carole Harris, Lesley Cottrell, and James Burns. "Risk and Protective Factors Associated with Gang Involvement Among Urban African American Adolescents." *Youth and Society* 34, no. 2 (2002): 172–194.

Lincoln, C. Eric, and Lawrence H. Mamiya. *The Black Church in the African American Experience*. Durham, N.C.: Duke University Press, 1990.

Martin, Elmer P., and Joanne Mitchell Martin. *The Black Extended Family*. Chicago: The University of Chicago Press, 1978.

Mason, S. "Pharisees." In *Dictionary of New Testament Background*. Edited by Craig A. Evans and Stanley E. Porter. Downers Grove, Ill.: InterVarsity Press, 2000.

McKinnon, Jesse. "The Black Population in the United States: March 2002." U.S. *Census Bureau*. Washington, D.C.: U.S. Department of Commerce, 2003. http://www.census.gov/prod/2003pubs/p20–541.pdf

Meredith, Martin. *The Fate of Africa: From the Hopes of Freedom to the Heart of Despair*. New York: PublicAffairs, 2005.

Meyers, Carol L. "Everyday Life: Women in the Period of the Hebrew Bible." In *Women's Bible Commentary*. Edited by Carol Newsom and Sharon H. Ringe. Louisville, Ky.: Westminster John Knox Press, 1998.

Meyers, Eric M., and James F. Strange. *Archaeology, The Rabbis, and Early Christianity*. Nashville: Abingdon Press, 1981.

Minkler, Meredith, KM Roe, and M. Price. "The Physical and Emotional Health of Grandmothers Raising Grandchildren in the Crack Cocaine Epidemic." *The Gerontologist* 32, no. 6 (1992): 752.

Mitchem, Stephanie. *Introducing Womanist Theology*. Maryknoll, N.Y.: Orbis Books, 2002.

Mobley, Mamie Till, and Christopher Benson. *Death of Innocence: The Story of the Hate Crime that Changed America*. New York: Random House, 2003.

Morris, Jerome. "What Does Africa Have to Do with Being African American?: A Microethnographic Analysis of a Middle School Inquiry on Africa." *Anthropology and Education Quarterly* 34, no. 3 (2003): 255–76.

National Clearinghouse on Child Abuse and Neglect Information. "Foster Care National Statistics." Washington, D.C.: U.S. Department of Health and Human Services, 2003. http://nccanch.acf.hhs.gov/pubs/factsheets/foster.cfm

Peskowitz, Miriam. "Families in Antiquity: Evidence from Tannaitic Literature and Roman Galilean Architecture." In *The Jewish Family in*

Antiquity. Edited by Shaye J. D. Cohen. Atlanta, Ga.: Scholars Press; Brown Judaic Studies, 1993.

Pierce, Robert. "Thoughts on Interpersonal Violence and Lessons Learned." *Journal of Interpersonal Violence* 20, no. 1 (2005): 43–50.

Pinn, Anthony B. *The Black Church in the Post–Civil Rights Era*. Maryknoll, N.Y.: Orbis Books, 2002.

Poku, Nana, and Fanta Cheru. "The Politics and Debt in Africa's AIDS Crisis." *International Relations* 15, no. 6 (2001): 37–54.

Pollock, Susan. "Bureaucrats and Managers, Peasants and Pastoralists, Imperialists and Traders: Research on the Uruk and Jemdet Nasr Periods in Mesopotamia." *Journal of World Prehistory* 6, no. 3 (1992).

Ramirez–Valles, Jesus, Marc A. Zimmerman, and Lucia Juarez. "Gender Differences of Neighborhood and Social Control Processes: A Study of the Timing of First Intercourse Among Low–Achieving, Urban, African American Youth." *Youth and Society* 33, no. 3 (2002): 418–441.

Reed, Jonathan L. *Kingdom Building in Galilee*. Claremont, Calif.: Institute for Antiquity and Christianity, 2002.

————.*The Population of Capernaum*. Claremont, Calif.: Institute for Antiquity and Christianity, 1992.

Reinhartz, Adele. "Parents and Children: A Philonic Perspective." In *The Jewish Family in Antiquity*. Edited by Shaye J. D. Cohen. Atlanta, Ga.: Scholars Press; Brown Judaic Studies, 1993.

Reisner, R. "Archaeology and Geography." In *Dictionary of Jesus and the Gospels*. Edited by Joel B. Green, Scot McKnight, and I. Howard Marshall. Downers Grove, Ill.: InterVarsity Press, 1992.

Reuters. "African Union Accuses Sudan in Darfur." *The New York Times*. 2 October 2005.

Richter, Mary Dee. "Statistics on Runaways: Florida Network on Youth and Family Services 2004 Report. Tallahassee, Fla.: Florida Network on Youth and Family Services, 2004. http://www.floridanetwork.org/NRPM–05/Statistics_on_Runaways.pdf

Riverside Church. "Power in the Pews: A Call to Action. The Crisis in Africa." December 2005.

Rodgers, Ph.D., Laura. "Meaning of Bereavement Among Older African American Widows." Geriatric Nursing 25, no.1 (2004): 10–15.

Royce, David D., and Gladys T. Turner. "Strengths of Black Families: A Black Community's Perspective." Social Work 25, no. 5 (1980): 407–409.

Satlow, Michael. "Reconsidering the Rabbinic Ketubah Payment." In The Jewish Family in Antiquity. Edited by Shaye J. D. Cohen. Atlanta, Ga.: Scholars Press; Brown Judaic Studies, 1993.

Saulny, Susan. "Storm and Crisis: the Displaced; Cast from Their Ancestral Home, Creoles Worry About Culture's Future." The New York Times, 11 October 2005, A15. http://select.nytimes.com/gst/abstract.html?res=F7091EFD3D5B0C728 DDDA90994DD404482

Sawatzky, Wendy. "Sudan's Lost Boys." Canadian Broadcasting Company, 4 May 2005. http://www.cbc.ca/manitoba/features/sudan

Schjonberg, Mary Frances. "Out of Deep Waters: New Orleans Kids Find a Place in Newark." Episcopal News Service, 28 October 2005. http://www.episcopalchurch.org/3577_68998_ENG_HTM.htm

Schmidt, T.E. "Taxes." In Dictionary of Jesus and the Gospels. Edited by Joel B. Green, Scot McKnight, and I. Howard Marshall. Downers Grove, Ill.: InterVarsity Press, 1992.

Shimkin, Demitri, Edith M. Shimkin, and Dennis A. Frate. The Extended Family in Black Societies. Berlin, Germany: Mouton De Gruyter, 1978.

Smith, Daniel L. "The Politics of Ezra: Sociological Indicators of Post-Exilic Judaean Society." In *Second Temple Studies I: Persian Period*. Edited by Philip R. Davies. Sheffield, England: Sheffield Academic Press, 1991.

Smith, R. Drew, ed. *Long March Ahead: African American Churches and Public Policy in Post–Civil Rights America (Public Influences of African American Churches)*. Durham, N.C.: Duke University Press, 2004.

Speller, Julia. *Walkin' the Talk: Keepin' the Faith in Africentric Congregations*. Cleveland: Pilgrim Press, 2005.

Spellman, William. *Addressing Community Gang Problems: A Practical Guide*. Edited by John Stedman and Deborah Lamm Weisel. Washington, D.C.: Bureau of Justice Assistance, 1998. http://www.ncjrs.gov/pdffiles/164273.pdf

Strange, James F. Edited by David Noel Freedman. "Nazareth." *Anchor Bible Dictionary*, Volume 4. New York: Doubleday, 1992.

Taylor, Robert Joseph, and Linda M. Chatters. "Religious Life." Chp. 6 in *Life in Black America*, edited by James S. Jackson, 105. Newberry Park, Calif.: Sage Publications, 1991.

Taylor, Robert Joseph, Linda M. Chatters, and James S. Jackson. "A Profile of Familial Relations Among Three–Generation Black Families." *Family Relations* 42 (1993): 341–352.

Taylor, Ronald, and Debra Roberts. "Kinship Support and Maternal and Adolescent Well–Being in Economically Disadvantaged African–American Families." *Child Development* 66, no. 6 (1995): 1585–1597.

Teicher, Stacy. "One New Orleans Family's New Life Far Away." *Christian Science Monitor* 22 September 2005. http://www.csmonitor.com/2005/0922/p01s04–lihc.html

Teplin, Ph.D., Linda A., Karen M. Abram, Ph.D., Gary M. McClelland, Ph.D., Mina K. Dulcan, Ph.D., and Amy A. Mericle, Ph.D., "Psychiatric Disorders in Youth in Juvenille Detention." *Archives of General Psychiatry* 59 (December 2002): 1133.

Thomas, Linda E., ed. *Living Stones in the Household of God: The Legacy and Future of Black Theology*. Minneapolis, Minn.: Augsburg Fortress Publishers, 2004.

Tierney, Joseph, J. B. Grossman, and N. L. Resch. *Making a Difference: An Impact Study of Big Brothers/Big Sisters*. Philadelphia: Public/Private Ventures, 1995.

Timberlake, Elizabeth M., and Sandra Stukes Chipungu. "Grandmotherhood: Contemporary Meaning Among African American Middle–Class Grandmothers." *Social Work* 37, no.7 (1992): 26.

"Timeline: Rwanda." *British Broadcasting Company*. October 12, 2005 http://news.bbc.co.uk/2/hi/africa/country_profiles/1070329.stm

Tolnay, Stewart E. *The Bottom Rung: African American Family Life on Southern Farms*. Champaign, Ill.: University of Illinois Press, 1999.

Townes, Emilie M., ed. *A Troubling in My Soul: Womanist Perspectives on Evil and Suffering*. Maryknoll, N.Y.: Orbis Books, 1993.

————.*Embracing the Spirit: Womanist Perspectives on Hope, Salvation and Transformation*. Maryknoll, N.Y.: Orbis Books, 1997.

UNICEF. "The Lost Boys of the Sudan." http://www.unicef.org/sowc96/closboys.htm

United Methodist Committee on Relief. "A Closer Look at Sudanese Refugee Resettlement." *UMCOR UPDATE: A Newsletter About the United Methodist Committee on Relief* 9, no. 1 (2001). http://gbgm–umc.org/umcor/update/lostboys.stm

U.S. Census Bureau. "Census 2000 Demographic Profile Highlights." *American FactFinder, Zip Code Tabulation Area* 48206. http://factfinder.census.gov/servlet/SAFFFacts?_event=Search&geo_id= 01000US&_geoContext=01000US&_street=&_county=&_cityTown=&_s tate=&_zip=48206&_lang=en&_sse=on&ActiveGeoDiv=geoSelect&_us eEV=&pctxt=fph&pgsl=010&_submenuId=factsheet_1&ds_name=DEC _2000_SAFF&_ci_nbr=null&qr_name=null&reg=null%3Anull&_keywor d=&_industry=

U.S. Department of State. "Trafficking in Persons Report. http://www.state.gov/g/tip/rls/tiprpt/2005/

Westerholm, S. "Pharisees." In *Dictionary of Jesus and the Gospels*. Edited by Joel B. Green, Scot McKnight, and I. Howard Marshall. Downers Grove, Ill.: InterVarsity Press, 1992.

White, Esq., James E., and Jean–Gontran Quenum, MBA. *Roots Recovered!: The How to Guide for Tracing African–American and West Indian Roots Back to Africa and Going There for Free or on a Shoestring Budget*. Bangor, Maine: Booklocker.com, 2004.

Wiedemann, Thomas. *Adults and Children in the Roman Empire*. New Haven, Conn.: Yale University Press, 1989.

Williams, Delores S. *Sisters in the Wilderness: The Challenge of Womanist God–Talk*. Maryknoll, N.Y.: Orbis Books, 1995.

Williams, Heather Andrea. *Self–Taught: African American Education in Slavery and Freedom*. Chapel Hill, N.C.: The University of North Carolina Press, 2005.

Williams, Juan, and Quinton Dixie. *This Far By Faith: Stories from the African American Religious Experience*. New York: Blackside, Inc., HarperCollins, 2003.

Williams, Krystal. *How to Plan Your African–American Family Reunion*. New York: Citadel Press, Kensington Publishing Corp, 2000.

Williams, Mary. *Brothers in Hope: The Story of the Lost Boys of Sudan*. Illustrated by R. Gregory Christie. New York: Lee & Low Books, 2005.

Wilmore, Gayraud. *Pragmatic Spirituality: The Christian Faith Through an Africentric Lens*. New York: New York University Press, 2004.

Wilson, Amos N. *The Developmental Psychology of the Black Child*. New York: Africana Research Center Publications, 1978.

Wordleman, Amy L. "Everyday Life: Women in the Period of the New Testament." In *Women's Bible Commentary*. Edited by Carol Newsom and Sharon H. Ringe. Louisville, Ky.: Westminster John Knox Press, 1998.

Wright Jr., Jeremiah A., and Colleen Birchett. *Africans Who Shaped Our Faith*. Chicago: Urban Ministries, 1995.

Yamauchi, E.. "Synagogue." In *Dictionar– of Jesus and the Gospels*. Edited by Joel B. Green, Scot McKnight, and I. Howard Marshall. Downers Grove, Ill.: InterVarsity Press, 1992.

Yarbrough, Larry O. "Parents and Children in the Jewish Family of Antiquity." In *The Jewish Family in Antiquity*. Edited by Shaye J. D. Cohen Atlanta, Ga.: Scholars Press, Brown Judaic Studies, 1993.

Yoffee, Norman, "Political Economy in Early Mesopotamian States." *Annual Review of Anthropology* 24 (1995): 281–311.

Zukeran, Patrick. "Archaeology and the New Testament." Probe Ministries. www.probe.org/content/view/30/77/